The Prep Group

by Eloisa Hope

Paperback	978-1-80369-485-6	
Hardback	978-1-80369-486-3	
Ebook	978-1-80369-487-0	

www.newgeneration-publishing.com

 New Generation Publishing

Disclaimer: This is a work of fiction. Any resemblance to persons living or dead is purely coincidental.

To my wife and our children, my whole world.
With all my love.

Foreword

"I will not stand by and witness another set of well intentioned, compassionate, hopeful adults slowly be destroyed by a system which fails to identify the real needs of traumatised children and then a few years later blames the inevitable disruption and breakdowns on the adoptive parents. It is systemic abuse. I've seen too much of it already." (Oakwater, H. 2017)[1].

This is a novel about contemporary adoption and while it may have been inspired by my own experiences, it is a work of fiction.

After falling in love with my adopted son, I wrote this novel while impatiently waiting for our adoption order to be granted and legally confirm what we already knew – that we were a forever family. My wife and I had experienced an arduous adoption process to reach that point, and it occurred to me that few novels featuring adoption covered the whole range of experiences. In writing this, I hoped to bridge that gap.

Primarily, I wanted to write a novel that I would have liked to read before I adopted. A fictional account that would make me laugh, cry, and empathise with the characters. A story I could enjoy, and a light-hearted read to break up the heavy attachment theory tomes on my adoption reading list, but which nonetheless informed me of what I might expect.

And so, *The Prep Group* was born.

Although entirely fictional, many situations that the characters experience were inspired by my personal journey

---

[1] Oakwater, Helen <u>Don't assume keeping a sibling group together is right</u> (2017).

to a family, as well as the many inspirational adoptive parents (and their incredible children) whom my wife and I met along the way. I wouldn't be the mother I am today to my beautiful boy – or the writer I have become – without the unparalleled support of the exceptional adopters who went before me, and my immense gratitude goes out to them all. (I'm looking at you #ukadoptioncommunity!) My characters experience infertility, IVF (both home and abroad), miscarriage, involuntary childlessness, the adoption approval process and adoption breakdown throughout the novel. It also features parents who choose adoption first.

When writing, I was aware that much of the story content would echo the experience of many families who came to adoption via infertility. However, adoption breakdown is a more exceptional experience, and it is for this reason that I write this foreword. Adoption disruption is the term used to describe an adoption that is ended by the parents (or, more rarely, the child's social worker) due to the adoption being deemed unsuccessful. This can take place either before or after the adoption order is granted.

Although relatively uncommon, figures suggest that approximately 3% of UK adoptions break down although statistics on this are not formally collected, suggesting the figure could be higher. Adoption disruption is rarely spoken about, so much so that it is almost taboo in the adoption community.

When we were going through it, our social workers were surprised when we told them we had connected with two couples who had also experienced a partial disruption (when one child stays with you but the other leaves the placement).

The way our social workers spoke to us about our experience often isolated us, discouraged us from seeking support, and made us feel as though we were the only ones. We were prevented from talking honestly about our grief. When grieving, you are encouraged to seek help and solace in others, but you feel like hiding away and keeping quiet in this particular grief. But determined not to let this break us, we found others. We sought out help through an adoption disruption support group, and there we found many heart-breaking real-life stories of incredible, ordinary people trying to take on extraordinary challenges.

Loving, kind, dedicated, committed adopters – just like all adopters.

The difference is that these wonderful parents chose to offer a family to children whose ability to live in a family was impacted long before they came to adoption. Repeatedly criticised and demonised by the system that had let them down, these adopters, who never had anything but the children's best interests at heart, are often left heartbroken. They suffer from depression, anxiety, secondary trauma and compassion fatigue, and can be cut off by friends and family who don't understand. They have lost their child, and therefore lost their whole world. They often speak of their lives having been ruined.

They are good people who tried their very best to fight for the best for their children, refusing to let this ruin them. This is why I chose to write this story featuring good people fighting to obtain the best outcomes within a system that doesn't seem to understand them. I wrote it to raise awareness of adoption disruption, and through my characters, to show that adoption is never straightforward. It can often be messy and complicated. But behind the struggle, there are so many stories filled with incredible, redemptive, and resilient love that overcomes it all.

Please note that although this novel deals with the topic of adoption disruption, it does not intend in any way to suggest that adoption of older children cannot work and shouldn't be considered. Adoption for children of all ages can be a fantastic way of providing a child with a permanent family. But every adoption story is different, and this novel portrays just a few of the many potential outcomes of that journey. As the author, I am very aware that there are many other potential, happy outcomes too. However, given the experiences I have had, I felt it important to tell a story in which other avenues for looked-after children are explored, highlighting the amazing work that is done by foster carers to keep vulnerable children safe.

The character of Tegan represents many older children in foster care for whom adoption may not be the right option. Unable to live safely with birth family, yet fiercely loyal to them; experiencing the effects of trauma from their early life experiences, yet unable to completely let go of the dream of reconciliation. For many children like Tegan, therapeutic foster carers do a vital job in supporting them while they work through their often-distressing early life experiences and preparing them for their future, which may or may not include birth family contact.

There are so many heart-warming stories within adoption, as well as challenges. As my character Alice says in the book, adoption is amazing. We wouldn't be a family without adoption, and as I sit here with my beautiful son by my side, I will never not be immensely grateful for the gift that is him.

I hope this book shows all of the love, beauty, and gifts that adoption can bring to families, as well as some of the challenges. While writing the stories of Adrian and Michael, Alice and George, Becka and Charlie, and those of the supporting characters in their lives, I hoped to show all the emotions they share as they grow to love the children in their care. They are not superheroes; they are simply ordinary people with big hearts. They make mistakes, they try their best, and they love with everything they've got.

Thank you for reading, and enjoy!

In the Beginning

In the beginning, there was the becoming.
You were there with me, holding my hand along each step
of the way.
My cheerleaders, how I needed you to hold me up.

And, in the end, there was the unbecoming.

To unbecome a mother to a child is the most heart-breaking
thing in the world, but I had to do it, for the child. Knowing
it was for the best.

But still my heart shattered like glass on the floor.

I fought for it, then gave it back.
I unbecame a mother.
I will never be one again.

This is my story.

Preface

"Mothers, I believe, intoxicate us. We idolize them and take them for granted. We hate them and blame them and exalt them more thoroughly than anyone else in our lives. We sift through the evidence of their love, reassure ourselves of their affection and its biological genesis. We can steal and lie and leave and they will love us." (Megan Mayhew Bergman, 2012[2])

We huddle in the cabin at the bottom of the garden, safe, warm and dry as the rain soaks the grass around us, beating angrily against the windows. In time with the rain, my little girl beats her feet on the floor as her fury rages, surpassing the storm outside.

Emotions swell between us, and my heart aches knowing that I'm the only one who knows this will be our last evening calling each other family. My last evening as Mummy, and her last evening trying and failing to see me as such.

It's been forty minutes now, and she's still screaming, her face red, eyes popping, and her expression contorting in distress. She knows her anger is being left to burn itself out in a safe place, instead of resulting in her demands being granted, but this realisation only results in more fury because, in this confused state, she doesn't know what it is she wants anymore.

Any attempted intervention from me results in further escalation, so I take a deep breath and try to remain calm.

She looks at me in desperation, begging me to help. I'm going to get my big voice out now, and you won't like it. I'm not going to stop screaming until you let me have what I want, but what she is yearning for, and cannot accept in the

---

[2] Mayhew Bergman, Megan. *Birds of a Lesser Paradise.* (2012)

present, is the love and care she was never given only a few years before.

So, I'm not going to back down because it will not help her. I hold my ground and give her space, trying to find enough calm inside me for both of us. The anger must work its way out.

When, as it always does, the anger subsides, we work through it. I state what happened clearly and I repeat it to help her brain make sense of what is real and not.

Trying to muddle through the trauma in her brain – the understanding of consequences, of routine.

I turned off the television at 5:30 p.m. like we do every day after ten, five and two-minute warnings.

Dinner was ready. It's the same routine every day, predictable and consistent. Just like the books tell you. Your food is getting cold, it's on the table waiting for you. Let's get inside.

The books don't tell you that sometimes predictability will result in emotional and behavioural regulation, and sometimes it won't.

On nights like tonight, you will find yourself in the midst of rages that last minutes, hours, or sometimes all night long.

You're mean and miserable, she shouts. You do these things to upset me. You want to hurt me.

The trauma narrative can be triggered at any time with no warning. Tonight is one of those nights.

If it were a one-off, if there were signs of improvement, some indication that we were breaking through, maybe we would be strengthened by it.

But none are shown.

The cabin may be safe, warm and dry, but the trauma cannot see that. We sit closely so that my daughter is safe by my side the whole time, but she looks at me in fear. Fear of the past, of memories, fear of what a family means. For her, family meals are not a place of comfort but a threat to be avoided at all costs.

Fight or flight kicks in, and the next thing I hear is that she's not feeling settled, or safe, here with us. You see, I don't want to live in your house and follow your rules. She pushes and spurns us, rejecting the rules put in place to keep her safe and regulated. We tried to keep the trauma away, but it kept getting in.

So, we sit. And the repetition sinks in – yes, your dinner is ready on the table. Yes, we always feed you. Yes, you're safe. No, there's no threat here.

The fight eventually falls away, and the calm returns, but it's a struggle to get there.

We sit and listen to the patter of rain outside. Our home is still standing. I know it feels to you as though we have run through the fire, but it's just the early evening routine at home. Safe. Together.

We're not the monsters you think we are, I think to myself.

She tells me she suffers from intense anger and she's scared. It makes her want to hurt herself and others. She asks us to help her, and I have to look away. I can't tell her that we've been crying down the phone for help all week from local authority social services. Our hope has faded as we've witnessed this little girl's descent into crisis, confusion and trauma. We know there is no help on offer and don't know where else to turn. Psychotherapy, a proper intervention, anything, she just needs something – we cry.

But these are only available once you've worked your way up through the hierarchy of support. It starts with therapeutic parenting in the home, we're told. But how do we begin when she is in crisis? we ask.

We say quietly, we've tried.

We don't know, but neither do they. We are the adoptive parents. We are meant to be the answer, the happy ever after.

But how can we be if the support we need never materialises? What becomes of the happy ending if returning our much-wanted child to the state's care is the only way to get the help she needs?

She looks me in the eyes and asks me to help, and my heart breaks, knowing that I can't.

Alice

NOW

'Tegan Rose.'

The silver and gold door plaque bearing her name had gone up in pride of place on the fresh gloss. The last of the finishing touches to her daughter's bedroom.

Her daughter. Alice whispered the word tentatively to herself, barely able to say it out loud for fear all this would disappear. She was still waiting for someone to wake her up, tell her she was dreaming.

It had certainly felt like a dream when they arrived home, stumbling into the house from matching panel just two weeks before, giggly from excitement and champagne, high on life and everything that was to come.

George, Alice's husband, told her to close her eyes and had disappeared into the pantry, reappearing with a mug engraved with *'Mummy'*, along with some flowers and chocolates, as tears welled in Alice's eyes. Knowing what the tears meant, George didn't need to say anything. He just hugged her tight as she wept softly.

Mummy. One precious word that held so much hope.

Delighted with it, Alice drank her coffee in the mug every morning from then on. She loved to wander around the house dreamily in her pyjamas and gown, cradling her coffee, while putting the finishing touches to her daughter's playroom and bedroom. Marvelling at the reality that she had finally found herself here on adoption leave, preparing to be a mum.

Alice's childhood dreams had always involved images of her floating around in nightwear with a big, glorious bump, while tiny feet and fists sporadically pushed out from the inside, a 'hello' against her skin. Alice would have giggled, 'Look, she wants to join the conversation!'

She longed to meet up with friends on lazy days of early maternity leave, pack her hospital bag with care, and await the magical day they would race to the hospital for the baby to arrive.

This dream had changed over the years, not by choice but by necessity. Still, now she had finished work to become an adopter, she felt content. Since matching panel day, the house had filled with flowers, gifts and cards from loved ones. Alice felt as cherished as she imagined she would have been as the proud owner of a baby bump.

Every morning she woke up feeling like the luckiest woman in the world, cuddling her husband before enjoying a whole day with no work. Her time was spent online shopping, cleaning and folding new clothes into paper-lined drawers. She was nesting and loving it. She felt blissful when she thought about the coming year, stretching ahead of her with infinite possibilities – a whole year learning to be a mum.

Setting down her coffee that morning, Alice had opened the eagerly awaited package that dropped on to the doormat with a soft thump as she finished her breakfast. Alice marvelled at the hand-crafted door plaque with her new daughter's name on it, lovingly swaddled in rainbow tissue paper. She swallowed hard, holding back a flood of emotion as she allowed herself to accept that a beautiful just-turned five-year-old girl would very soon call her Mummy.

She smiled as she remembered the day George had arrived home on a Friday night from work. Instead of the usual white wine and a takeaway, he carried pots of paint and new brushes. 'Let's do this!' he'd announced, a wry smile on his lips as he presented her with the 'sunshine yellow' shade he'd chosen.

Alice had quickly changed into an old t-shirt and overalls, tied her red hair up in a messy bun and got to work painting the empty spare bedroom.

It was one of those snapshot moments she would treasure forever, painting their new baby's room together. She took lots of photos for Instagram to immortalise this milestone, splashing paint on her husband's clean white shirt. Smiling, she saved the photos to upload later to share with her adopter friends, impatient to see their reactions.

Alice was an active member of the adoption community on Instagram and had shared her adoption journey with her hundreds of followers. Many were former IVF friends who cheered with her when she received the much-longed-for 'BFPs' (positive pregnancy test results) and helped her to remain hopeful through each anxious two-week-wait. They kept up her spirits when she was low and mourned with her during each miscarriage. Announcing they'd been approved to adopt had been met with hundreds of supportive comments. The community was invaluable to Alice, although George didn't understand it at all. He didn't get on with social media, as he never understood why anyone would want to put their life on show for a 'bunch of strangers'. Yet, he still grudgingly posed for photos, holding up milestone cards every step of the way, and always smiled for the camera. He must love her, she thought, smiling to herself.

To Alice, her online friends were anything but strangers. Meeting a group of like-minded friends who understood the ups and downs of building a family was wonderful. They knew how a pregnancy announcement from a friend could completely ruin your day without having to explain it, and that meant so much.

George was a good man. And yes, of course he had faults, but he was a good husband. The strong, silent type, Alice mused. He looked for solutions rather than talking about his feelings but, Alice reasoned, that's men for you. George was practical, trustworthy, reliable and an excellent son-in-law, much loved by his and her family alike. He worked hard at his accountancy job during the week, but was committed to his down-time at the weekend, doing jobs around the house, spontaneously suggesting they go out for brunch and loving long walks through the woods with their excitable labradoodle, Mitch.

George worked hard, but left work at work and home at home. Life was straightforward for him, she thought.

Alice's mind wandered to the congratulations card they'd received through the post this morning. A gorgeous illustration of two parents and a child on the front, hand-drawn by one of their creative friends, with a message inside written in quirky script: *'So pleased for you both – you deserve this so much!'*

Alice had flinched involuntarily at the inscription and almost let the card fall from her shaking hands. She shuddered as the words triggered unwelcome memories, clouding her thoughts. Unthinkingly, Alice stroked the pale, white scars on her wrist. She was gripped by the pounding of her heart, something she experienced every time these memories emerged, and she gasped to catch her breath. Breathing deeply into her belly, as she'd been taught, Alice fought to regain control of her feelings.

'Axel can't hurt me now,' she whispered to herself, pushing away the panicky feelings prickling at her scalp as dark memories of her ex-boyfriend filled her thoughts.

So immersed was she in these thoughts that the ping of her phone startled her, her pulse jumping into her throat. Taking a deep breath, Alice went to open the text, still shaken by the shift in her mood. When these feelings re-emerged, even a well-meaning text from a friend felt like a threat, causing her palms to sweat and her breathing to become shallow. She knew it was unreasonable – it wasn't real, she was safe now – but it still took a while for her to look at the text from her friend, as if steeling herself for bad news. It wasn't.

The chirpy message was from Charlie:

'Morning, Mama! How are you doing? (still in bed enjoying a lie-in? And if not, why not?!) These are your last moments of freedom, so enjoy them! Stay in bed all day,

drink gin, go to the loo in peace!! Sod it, do all three at the same time, just because you can! Don't think of me mired in dirty nappies and regurgitated porridge 24/7 – love it really, ha ha. I don't think Becka's washed her hair in WEEKS, and I'm thinking of shaving my head completely to save me the job – that's my life now!! Thinking of you, hope you're doing great and enjoying the nesting :)'

Alice smiled. She and George had met Charlie (ex-social worker, very confident and familiar with the whole process) and her (achingly trendy, blue-haired, artist) wife, Becka, during their Stage 1 adoption training courses.

With some trepidation, they had all walked into the over-heated training room at the council offices that December, nervous about what the coming days would bring, and had filled the silence with awkward jokes and small talk. They'd got weak coffee from the machine (and complained about it) and fought over the stale chocolate biscuits on offer.

Four intensive days of training consisted of everything to do with early-life trauma: ACES (Adverse Childhood Experiences), PLACE (Playfulness, Love, Acceptance and Empathy), therapeutic parenting, a child's journey through foster care to adoption and more, all with a group of equally excited prospective parents known as their 'prep group' friends. Alice and George loved meeting a group of similarly minded people, all dedicated to becoming the best parents they could be. They'd loved watching as the other couples had become misty-eyed during the training videos and clutched each other's hands tightly during the challenging parts of the day, which had addressed the traumatic experiences many children in care had.

Over coffee, during their breaks, the couples had chatted openly, with the emotionally charged nature of the day causing them to open up quickly about their stories. Stumbling over their words, they laughed nervously as their experiences spilt out and overlapped. Everyone was happy to be amongst others who understood what it was like to be an adopter, without having to explain. It was their equivalent of the NCT baby groups that expectant parents become a part of, and the support it provided was invaluable.

One of the social worker trainers who presented during the four-day course was funny, likeable and realistic about the adopters' challenges. Alice really warmed to her. Her name was Sami. Alice was delighted once their training was over, and she and George had passed panel, to find that Sami was the children's worker for Tegan and would work with them to get their daughter home.

At the end of her presentation, Sami looked at them all and said with a memorable directness, 'Trust your gut. If a match feels right to you, it could be the right one, but if there's anything that doesn't feel right, don't ignore it. Speak out. Tell us how you're feeling. We can only get the match right if you talk to us, and if you're honest with us. This is the future of *your* family, so let us work with you to get it as right for everyone as we can.'

Sami was a family finder and Alice loved the idea of that phrase. After all of this time, the thought of having a 'family finder' working with her to form her forever family was everything she'd ever hoped for.

But trusting her gut was not something Alice was used to doing. Her gut instinct had let her down many times before and she could only hope that this time it would be right.

Sami

NOW

My feet hurt, thought Sami, as she trudged up the stairs to her cramped office, towards her small desk covered, as it always was, in paperwork. A cold coffee sat next to her computer with half a packet of crisps (a.k.a. lunch) that she'd been eating before she'd been called out on an emergency visit to a family in early placement struggling with their child's behaviour as they settled into their new home. Now, an online training course with a disappointing 2% completed notification blinked into sight as Sami nudged the mouse, bringing the computer screen back to life. That was optimistic, thought Sami, as she sighed and ran a nail-bitten hand through her short spiky hair. She knew that thinking she would ever get the time to complete the continuing professional development that she was supposed to do as an early-career social worker was unrealistic.

No task was ever completed uninterrupted in this job. There was always something that took precedence, some emergency visit, call or meeting that Sami had to attend. Late nights were non-negotiable in order to complete all of the reports and other paperwork she had to fill in with alarming frequency. No matter how many early mornings she worked or late nights she stayed, the job never seemed to get easier or the workload any less, she mused. As well as sore feet, Sami had red eyes from a lack of sleep and a persistent headache from the caffeine she consumed every day to keep her focused. She dreamed of Friday night when she could close the door of her cosy flat, change into fluffy pyjamas, put her feet up and catch up on some television. She hadn't had a moment to relax this week.

Sami hoped she'd not forgotten to feed her cat, Munchkin, that morning, then remembered that the freezer was long overdue defrosting, and the food shopping hadn't been done. More jobs for the weekend. As it was, she'd be asleep on the sofa at 8 p.m. by the time the weekend came around, Sami thought.

Some Friday night that's going to be! And that's assuming she would be home from work by that time.

As a social worker in the child permanence team, Sami's job was to find families for the children in foster care who had been removed from families that could not look after them. Her favourite part of the job is when she meets prospective adopters during linking meetings in their homes as they begin creating a new family. Adopters are full of optimism and desperate to offer their love, beautiful homes and families to a child in need of just that. These are the moments that make all the hard work, paperwork, and stress worthwhile. This was why she went into social care. On days like these, when the job feels relentless and heart-breaking, these are the moments that keep her going.

As a former foster child who'd never had the chance to become part of an adoptive family, this work was close to Sami's heart. She was the child of a young, alcoholic mum, and was removed from her mother at birth, only to be returned, unsuccessfully, to her care after an appeal when Sami was two years old. From the notes Sami had read when she turned eighteen, a chaotic home life had ensued for the following five years. This resulted in Sami being returned to foster care at the age of seven. Too old to be considered for adoption at the time, she was placed in long-term foster care. Angry, traumatised and confused, Sami's behaviour spiralled, sabotaging the placement and resulting in three moves in two years.

Finally, at the age of ten, Sami had found herself in a long-term therapeutic foster care placement living with two older, experienced foster carers, Mary and John, who she credits with saving her life. They picked her up when she felt no one would love her enough to look past the anger and pain that she was so loudly expressing.

When she screamed, they stood by her and taught her to manage her anger, listening to her when she raged against the world. They liaised with school, putting in strategies to get her back on track with her education until finally, she left school at eighteen with a respectable list of qualifications.

When she turned eighteen, Mary and John encouraged her to read about her past and helped her make sense of it. They encouraged her to develop empathy for her birth mother and the circumstances that led her to make the choices she did. Sami's birth mother had sadly passed away by this time, she had no more children and Sami's birth father was unknown. Having no connections with her biological origins, Sami was left feeling rootless for a few years. She drifted for a while, she spent a few years working in unsatisfying jobs and struggled with her emotions. Yet still, one night, a conversation with Mary about her past ignited her passion for social care and pushed her to apply to become a social worker as a mature student.

Poring over books, reading case studies, talking about social care, understanding behaviour, and studying childhood trauma was a turning point for Sami. It was incredibly therapeutic and helped her come to terms with her past, understand herself, and develop a greater admiration for the dedication Mary and John had put into her life. It was thanks to them that she became the productive adult she is today. Even on the days when it was challenging and exhausting, Sami felt that training in social care was the best thing she'd ever done. She brought a deep understanding of the system to the role that many others couldn't and was proud of having achieved this professional status, given her difficult start in life.

It didn't mean that on days like this one, she didn't feel like going home and pouring herself a large gin, thought Sami, smiling. But that gin was going to have to wait, judging by the number of emails in her inbox, the number of voicemails that plagued her phone, and the file that had just arrived on her desk. She opened the file and smiled at the update. One of the children on her caseload, Tegan, had recently been matched with a couple of prospective adopters. This week the ADM (Agency Decision Maker) had ratified the matching panel's decision to proceed with introductions.

Sami was delighted at the news, and completely overjoyed for Tegan. In this little girl, she could see so much of her own story. Tegan was a charismatic, spirited girl who had gone through more in her short five years than many adults do in a lifetime. Charming, outspoken and confident – she had the spirit of a survivor.

The child of a young mother who had fallen into a deep depression following her escape from an abusive relationship, Tegan had been removed from her birth family at the age of three. She was dirty, undernourished and neglected, and had lived in foster care ever since. Now, Sami couldn't wait to see her settled in her new home and made a note to give the prospective parents a call this week to congratulate them on the ADM decision.

Sami had sat with Alice and George during the matching panel, fighting to maintain a professional demeanour as she listened to their emotional description of how they were enchanted by Tegan at their first 'bump-into' meeting that had taken place a few weeks before. The mum-to-be, Alice, had cuddled the transition toy meant for Tegan throughout the panel as she and George talked about how much they were looking forward to being parents to this cheeky, red-haired, feisty little girl. Not a dry eye could be seen amongst the panel members as they gave their unanimous 'yes' verdict.

Sami felt optimistic about this match and hoped that this would be the fairy-tale ending that everyone involved in the case was so desperately hoping for. Settling down to her work, she had a smile on her face for the rest of the day, despite the arduous Friday afternoon team meeting.

Finally, the meeting had finished, and Sami turned over her phone that was buzzing insistently next to her to see five missed calls flash up on the screen – two were from Peggy and three were from Piper. Ugh, not again, they can wait, Sami thought irritably. Right now, it was time to focus on Tegan's new family.

Sami felt in her bones that something exciting was happening for this little girl. And she was a part of making a new family's future truly great, which is the best feeling in the world.

Adrian

NOW

'Don't worry,' Sami had said, her hand on Adrian's arm imparting little reassurance. 'It will all come together, you'll see. I'll chase up the play therapy and your social worker will call you soon. It's still early days. You've got so much adjusting to do. Take care of yourselves, get some sleep, and everything will seem better in the morning!' And with that she left with a brief wave, off to her next appointment.

Adrian called goodbye to Sami as she waved from the end of the path, then closed the door and sank down into a chair, running a hand over his face. Exhausted and drained, he yearned for sleep. He couldn't remember the last time he'd taken a shower and had the theme tune of *Paw Patrol* on repeat in his head – it was the only thing that worked to calm his little boy, Joey. The double-shot coffee from the machine his husband, Michael, bought him last year wasn't touching Adrian's fatigue today. He hid in the kitchen to raid the hidden chocolate stores, but this only escalated things when Joey saw the wrappers in the bin and threw himself on the floor in protest, banging his head. Adrian had tried and failed to soothe him as his limbs flailed angrily.

There was nothing he could do but take deep breaths, trying to establish some internal calm before going into the playroom again.

Ear-splitting screaming echoed inside his head, and his stress levels were rising. He knew that he needed to co-regulate with the unhappy child currently screaming and throwing all of his Lego against the wall. Still, at this moment, he needed five minutes of calm.

Joey had just turned three years old and had been placed with Adrian and Michael for adoption four months before.

The whole family was overjoyed at his arrival and the early days of being a family; however, it soon became apparent that Joey's needs were more significant than Adrian or Michael realised, and they were struggling to adjust to becoming parents overnight to a child they had to work so hard to understand.

Suspected to have been exposed to drugs while in the womb and neglected while a small baby, Joey's ability to regulate was compromised and his meltdowns were difficult to manage. It was taking its toll on both men who were trying everything in a bid to help their boy settle into his new home.

Adrian and Michael were successful in their chosen careers, Adrian as a conveyancing solicitor and Michael as a deputy head in a primary school. They worked long hours for many years at the beginning of their relationship to enjoy the kind of lifestyle they had always dreamed of. A beautiful, detached home in the countryside, a garden full of apple and pear trees, four chickens in a coop at the bottom of the garden providing them with fresh eggs every day, and two pampered Siamese cats who ruled the house.

The two men had enjoyed two holidays a year since they became a couple ten years before, travelling all over the world. Once they both turned forty (with a huge, extravagant house party, the best champagne and many friends), their thoughts turned to parenthood.

Adrian had never wanted to be a dad until he met Michael. Knowing he was gay from the age of twelve, he'd always thought that parenthood was off the table for him. He'd enjoyed his life of hard work and luxury, earning a good salary and buying the things in life that he'd wanted.

His dream was the life he had been living before the thought of adoption crossed their minds. The excellent job, the beautiful home and garden, the holidays and most of all, the lovely husband who was his best friend. He hadn't dared hope for more. Michael pushed him to imagine himself as a father, and bit by bit, he began to see himself in that role.

As a primary school teacher, Michael was a nurturing, patient man who had always desperately wanted to be a father. Brought up in a large, loving family, his dream was to have two or three children and many pets filling a noisy, happy home.

Meeting the love of his life at the age of thirty only consolidated his dream of being a husband and a father. To him, adoption was the only route to parenthood. With a younger adopted sister that he adored, he had seen all of the positives that adoption can bring to a family. He couldn't wait to share everything he had in life with a child of his own.

The week before they'd attended their adoption approval panel, Adrian and Michael had been surprised with a call from their social worker. She wanted to ask if another worker from the child permanence team could give them a call that afternoon.

This was not usual practise, she said, but a profile had come in and they all felt this child could be the perfect match for Adrian and Michael. Slightly speechless – as they had not been approved yet and were not expecting to hear of a match for a few weeks, if not months – Michael had taken the call from Sami, who then emailed over a password-protected copy of Joey's profile. Adrian managed to come home early from work (on Michael's insistence), so that they could open the profile and read it together. Sami had made sure they were aware that nothing would progress until they had been approved. Still, if they thought they could be parents to this child, things could potentially move quite quickly after approval.

Quite quickly had been an understatement. Four months from the date of the approval panel, the ADM (Agency Decision Maker) approved the match between Adrian, Michael and Joey. Then two weeks later, after an intensive introduction period, Joey moved in.

Joey was absolutely adorable, with big brown eyes and a mop of curly brown hair. He was a ball of energy from the moment they met him. Two weeks of introductions passed in an exhausting blur of playdates, early mornings, late nights, very little sleep, and a flood of emotions. Every day, the two new dads took on more responsibility for this little boy in their care – feeding him, changing him and taking over the morning routine. They arrived in the early hours at the foster carer's house, heading upstairs to wake Joey up as the foster carer made them cups of strong coffee that never got finished. And on the last day they put Joey to bed at his foster carer's house, changing him into pyjamas after his bath and tucking him in with his blanket and teddy, which was an emotional moment for both of them.

Joey was three years old, but his failure to thrive brought on by his early life experiences had left him small for his age. He was as small as an eighteen-month-old, and in the low light, cuddled up with his blanket, sucking his thumb, he seemed as vulnerable as the tiniest of babies to his new dads. Placing a kiss on his forehead as his eyes began to close, they looked at each other, clasping hands tightly in the room softly lit by a child's nightlight.

They began to fall in love with this brave boy who put all his trust in them so easily. Driving home in the dark, they were barely able to talk, so lost in their own thoughts, knowing that the following day the introductions would now be made in their home. They were one step closer to being parents.

Adrian now sat on the playroom floor, watching Joey as he lay before him, screaming and writhing as if he were in pain. His little face was contorted with what looked like fury. Exhausted, Adrian felt like crying himself. This was not the first significant meltdown of the day. Their sleep had been disturbed by night terrors since Joey had moved in, and they knew this small child was going through so much grief that his dads felt helpless in the face of it. Any attempts to pick Joey up or console him resulted in kicking, struggling and fists to the face from the small boy. On one occasion, he flung his head back so hard in anger that Adrian ended up with a bloody nose. This distressed Joey even more, as Adrian tried to hold in his own feelings of pain to console his child.

Feelings of powerlessness threatened to overwhelm Adrian. He could do nothing but sit by his child and hold his hand as the trauma worked its way through the small boy's body. He tried to comprehend the sense of loss that the child was processing as he transferred his affections from the foster carer to his new dads. The enormity of what they had taken on brought tears to Adrian's eyes.

The children's books that they'd lovingly collected months before sat unread on the shelves, while the ones they had attempted to read had their pages shredded. The washing was piling up, the kitchen was a mess, Adrian and Joey had not managed to leave the house that day, and Adrian was counting the minutes until Michael came home to take over. To give him five minutes of quiet.

He looked down at his phone as Joey ran head-first at him, pummelling his chest with his small fists, his screaming now turning to exhausted sobs as he wore himself out. Adrian tried a tentative hand, gently placed on his head. This was soon shaken off with a very loud 'NO!' and the pummelling of Joey's small fists against his chest re-started.

Adrian's spirits lifted momentarily as a text came in from Michael but then dropped just as quickly when he read: *'So sorry, got to work late. Be home by seven. Will pick up takeaway! Love you, xx.'*

Adrian took in a deep breath. Sami's visit had left him feeling more alone and hopeless on difficult days like these. Adrian found it hard to accept her assurances that it would all get easier. This was just one small child. How could this be so hard? How is it that he couldn't cope with one child when other parents have three or four and look so on top of everything? How could he fail as a parent at the age of forty when so many young parents make it look so easy?

How he wished he could call on his mum for support, but that was never going to happen, he thought sadly.

Instead, Adrian scrolled to the Instagram community of adopters to search for support. The last time he'd posted an honest description of the problems he and Michael were facing with Joey, he'd received an outpouring of non-judgemental support.

His instinct had been telling him to struggle on, ashamed that he couldn't cope. But after chatting with other parents, he realised this wasn't helpful to him, Joey, or Michael. Holding in his worries around parenting was only causing his anxieties to rise. He realised that this online space was the community that really understood what it was like to be an adoptive parent, and knew the challenges that so many adopters lived with every day.

After scrolling through a few posts tagged #therapeuticparenting and picking up some practical advice, Adrian smiled. He took a deep breath and was ready to try again. Finding the bubble maker, he prepared his mindset for an afternoon of playfulness to help support his boy through this tricky time. He could do this. He could be the daddy this little boy needs, even if it took learning a whole new style of parenting to get there.

Alice

NOW

Alice enjoyed the pre-adoption training course so much more than she'd thought she would. One of the highlights was meeting the other prospective adopters, particularly Adrian and Michael, and Charlie and Becka.

Charlie and Becka were quirky and outspoken. Charlie's dry humour entertained the group during the ice-breaker sessions (making even George with his conservative sense of humour crack a smile at times) and Becka's extensive research before attending ('do I get a gold star?!' she'd laughed) made everyone feel like kids who hadn't done their homework. Alice, laughing, promised to read that book on therapeutic parenting sitting on the coffee table.

Ever the organiser, Alice had asked for everyone's contact details at the end of the course to set up the Prep Group WhatsApp to keep in touch. She was so glad she had overcome her naturally shy nature to do it. The friends she'd made, she hoped, would be friends for life. They were an essential part of the support network that they'd proudly discussed with their visiting social worker throughout the intensive assessment process.

Charlie and Becka had just recently had two-year-old twin boys placed with them and were in the 'cocooning' stage post-placement. As far as Alice understood, that had meant they'd been mostly staying at home in the new parent bubble. Meeting the children's needs, staying close to each other, forming attachments, and helping the children feel safe and secure in their new home as well as watching lots of *Peppa Pig*, clearing up spills, changing nappies and drinking wine once the blur of non-stop activity that was the twins had finally gone to bed. The photos Charlie and Becka had sent to their private WhatsApp group were fantastic, showing a united family only a few weeks in. To Alice, it sounded perfect. Charlie's often-hilarious texts about life as a new parent to the two 'eating-sleeping-pooping terrors' made Alice excited for what was to come. It was clear how much Charlie and Becka loved their two sons, even in this early stage, and it gave Alice so much hope for the loving relationship she hoped to build with her new daughter.

Excitedly, they'd called George's mum on the day they'd officially been linked with Tegan. They were over the moon and bursting to share the news with their loved ones. They chattered away happily until they paused for a moment to gauge her reaction, and then it hit them.

George's mum's response had been anything but warm, leaving Alice feeling deflated. George tried to smooth things over, but Alice couldn't shake the way the conversation made her feel and dwelled on it for days to follow.

Not understanding their choice to adopt an older child, her mother-in-law focused on potential difficulties without sharing in their excitement. But Alice felt they were going into it with their minds open. They'd done the research, they knew about therapeutic parenting, they'd attended the training. Sharing the news about their new child was meant to be an exciting time of celebration, and the shine of the moment had been dulled by George's mum's less than exuberant reaction. Of course, George promised to talk to his mum about it, but he also told Alice she was being over-sensitive. Still, after waiting such a long time to be a mummy, Alice wasn't going to let anything ruin this experience for her.

Yes, there was a part of Alice that longed for a sweet-smelling baby to love. To carry around close to her heart as a warm extension of her own body, her treasure in a baby-carrier, bonding from those early moments of life. So Alice understood why many people in her life, particularly those who had known her through infertility, were shocked to find that she and George weren't adopting a baby (which was called early permanence or foster to adopt). But the risk of the baby being returned to birth parents after you'd fallen in love with them was too much for Alice to contemplate. She'd had her heart broken more times than she could count, and was determined not to invite more heartache into her life.

And there was something about this girl. Browsing Linkmaker (the website displaying profiles of children waiting for adoption) Alice was struck by Tegan's cheeky grin. Tegan was described as 'a spirited tomboy' and loved playing outside, getting dirty and making people laugh. Alice couldn't help noticing that with her mass of wavy red hair, adorable gap-toothed smile and smattering of freckles, she physically resembled Alice's side of the family, particularly her lovely younger sister. She couldn't put her finger on it, but she knew this child was meant to be her daughter. She could feel it.

Adoption is amazing, Alice thought, grinning. What an incredible experience they had had so far, and it was only going to get better. This was her life now – great friends, a gorgeous husband, a beautiful home, and an incredible daughter on the way. The past couldn't touch her now. She was safe. Safe, happy and in love. And they were about to be parents.

Their future was about to start, and she couldn't wait. She'd fought so hard to get where she was now, and she wasn't about to let anything get in the way of her happy life. Alice snapped a quick photo of Tegan's new room and went downstairs to make a coffee. Later, she would post one of the images on Instagram, feeling full of love for her new daughter as she crafted the caption to go with the photo:

'First clothes have gone into the wardrobe! This has made my emotions go haywire and feels like such a massive moment in our journey. At the weekend, we went to George's sister's house to spend time with her and the children.

We left with a car full of second-hand clothes and toys for our girl – our precious daughter is being so spoiled already! George's sister filled up our car with bags full of beautiful girls' clothes, books, toys, as well as wine, chocolates, and a house plant for me. We've been inundated with congratulations on our panel approval, and we are so grateful for all of it! We've agreed to put away the clothes for now as we don't want to overwhelm our new daughter with too much new stuff in the beginning. Still, I couldn't resist hanging up a few cute clothes in LG's (little girl's) room as I've waited such a long time to do that. I also ordered my first online item for her – a pair of dungarees that will be perfect for playing outside in! I'm so excited to become a mummy and I'm really enjoying having this time to 'nest' in preparation for her arrival. Love to you all on your journeys! #ukadoptioncommunity x '.

Adrian

THEN

The music spills out in a rush onto the rain-washed street as Adrian and Michael push the heavy door of the city centre pub. They walk in smiling, hand-in-hand, shaking raindrops from their hair and pulling off their raincoats as they're hit by the warmth inside. Looking over at Michael, the glow of happiness exuding from his face, Adrian squeezes his hand and feels a rush of love for this wonderful man he married. He briefly thinks, *I would do anything for this man here*. He watches as Michael quickly scans the bustling room for the group of friends they're meeting, gently pulling Adrian's hand as he pushes through the crowd. Flushed with adrenaline, prosecco and the congratulations from their friends and family, the two men are looking forward to carrying on the celebrations with their prep group friends, the people who really get how much this means to them, and the life-changing enormity of what has just happened.

It's the Friday night following Adrian and Michael's matching panel, and the prep group friends are meeting for drinks in a recently opened gastropub, looking forward to trying the elaborate cocktails and positively reviewed tapas. *'We have to try it!'* Michael had texted, and everyone agreed. This meet-up has been long overdue. The WhatsApp group chat dragged out with endless dates that no one could do in the end. Finally, their matching panel, and the need to celebrate it, was an incentive to find a date that worked. Somehow, they're all free this Friday night and excited to see each other.

Alice and George arrived early and reserved a booth at the back of the pub, spreading their coats over the spare seats as they waited for their friends. Alice delightedly scans the menu for her favourite Baileys cocktail before sending

George to the bar to order it and his pint of beer. Charlie and Becka arrive shortly after, ordering a couple of bottles of wine, one white and one red. Drink and conversation flow freely as they all catch up on adoption news, and Charlie has brought a book with her that she thought Alice would enjoy. It's the latest edition of the therapeutic parenting manual that they had bonded over during prep training. They chat about that while George makes awkward small talk with Becka (small talk not being his forte).

None of the other adopters have had their children placed yet. Charlie and Becka are eagerly awaiting their boys' matching panel, and Alice and George are in the initial linking conversations about their little girl with the family finder team.

But the mood is still happy and excited. The friends are glad to be together again for the first time since they had coffee together, shell-shocked from information overload on the last day of the training course. Adrian and Michael eventually make it to the booth, and everyone shuffles over so they can sit down after the initial flurry of kisses and congratulations has been given all round.

Becka's cheeks are flushed with wine and the warmth of the pub as she reaches across the table to embrace Adrian and Michael in a hug. 'Congratulations, guys! You did it – you're going to be dads! How are you feeling?' She gushes warmly, kissing both men twice, once on each cheek.

'Because we're blummin' terrified,' chimes in Charlie with a laugh, raising her glass to the two men, actually looking anything but.

Adrian, happy to be amongst like-minded friends, pours himself a drink and lets Michael talk. He settles in for an evening enjoying the company of his friends, good wine and conversation.

Michael, the more talkative of the pair, has his hand on Adrian's knee while regaling the group with their matching panel experience. Smiling, he describes the adorable kids' clothes they've bought and the playroom they've decorated.

It all feels very surreal that this is finally happening. They are going to be dads after all this time. They are going to have a son.

Adrian watches as the rain beats against the windowpanes in the darkness outside and thinks, our relationship will never be the same again. From now on, we'll be parents. There will be three of us, and these times of just us are suddenly fleeting. He zones out of the conversation, and stares into his drink, lost in his thoughts.

The conversation flows smoothly, until Alice says quietly, 'But aren't you scared, though? I mean really, genuinely, just scared?'

Adrian looks up. Everyone looks at Alice and pauses a moment. Were they scared? Michael always seems so confident, so sure that everything will turn out well. But in his quiet moments, Adrian would admit to feeling something close to fear. They worked so very hard for this. They can't afford to fail. Months have been spent filling in workbooks, asking family and friends for references, going to training courses, meeting with social workers. Proving themselves to have the potential to be excellent parents because those are the parents these children need after everything they have been through.

Adrian has read the horror stories online when adoption goes wrong, and the adoptive parents can't cope. The results of childhood trauma and the impacts that can last throughout the children's lives, the times when love is not enough to heal the scars of the past.

Ever the academic, Adrian has read the research papers on attachment theory and knows all about the impact of adverse childhood experiences. Hoping to be as prepared as he could be for a child who needs him, he read everything possible before the panel. Still, now, rather than feeling prepared, he begins to feel overwhelmed at the potential challenges awaiting them. He's scared of that.

How could he parent well when his own experience of parenting had been so chaotic? Being a parent to an adopted child who needs consistency more than anything was a daunting prospect when all you'd ever known was upheaval.

But somehow, when Alice asks this, he can't find the words to express the complicated fears that rattle through his head. He laughs it off and joins the others in their banter about sleepless nights and cleaning up poo, and jokes about it not being too late to change their minds. Adrian then excuses himself from the table and pushes his way through the crowd to the bar, secretly hoping that no one will ever ask him if he wants to change his mind.

He doesn't trust himself not to.

Becka

NOW

'So, have you heard from Adey and Mike lately?'

Becka pottered around the homely kitchen making coffee with some difficulty, as she had one blond-haired toddler, Parker, hanging off her right leg. The other, Phoenix, was sitting in the middle of the flagstone kitchen floor, happily banging an overturned saucepan with a wooden spoon, like a makeshift drum. Both children were still dressed in their fleece pyjamas.

'*I'm* dressed, and we're all fed and watered, so I count that as a win this morning!' A yawning Becka had announced as she'd opened the door to Alice, while the twins hid behind her legs.

Alice set down the potted white rose and card that she'd bought for Charlie and Becka on the marble-topped island, and settled into the sofa in the corner of the farmhouse-style kitchen. She moved some brightly coloured cushions, and a handful of children's books and soft toys to make space. Becka, smiling, having refused Alice's offer to help with the coffee, gently extracted Parker from her leg and plopped him, slightly bemused, onto the sofa next to Alice. The little boy sat and stared at her, with his thumb firmly in his mouth, and his big blue eyes watching her every move.

'Hey, Parker!' Alice smiled, gently stroking his warm back with one hand, resisting the urge to pull the tiny toddler on to her lap for a cuddle, tempting as it was. He looked so cute and cuddly in his pyjamas, holding his toy tiger. Newly placed children needed to have their needs met by their parents in these early days. Alice's training had taught her this. It ensured that those primary attachments were formed before any other visiting friends or family had those precious first cuddles. So, for now, as this was the first time

Alice had visited Charlie and Becka's inner-city townhouse since the women had had their twins placed with them, Alice knew she'd have to settle for smiles and giggles instead of the cuddles she longed to give. Alice had been eagerly awaiting the chance to catch up with the new family, and lavishing some love on these beautiful little boys who had turned her friends' lives happily upside down.

In her self-deprecating way, Becka had told Alice that their social worker had said she wished all adopters were like her and Charlie. That they wanted to bottle whatever it was they were doing because they were getting it so right. 'Smug or what?!' Becka had laughed.

Alice hadn't found it smug at all. All she had felt had been a rush of admiration for her friends that they were making such a happy life for their two new children. But this was closely followed by the shadow of anxiety. What if she wasn't able to do this herself? What if, after all of this, it went wrong somehow? What if she let this new child down after everything they'd been through? Now she struggled to stay present as Becka chatted away, as insecurities rushed around inside her head, bubbling up every time she thought of the steep learning curve of learning to be a parent.

But one thing she couldn't help noticing was Becka's evident joy. It was in every move she made. It was clear that Becka and Charlie were loving adoption leave and being mums to their gorgeous new additions. They'd thrown themselves into new parenthood with enthusiasm. Even just a few months into placement, the fridge was covered with a gallery of colourful toddler artwork, many joyful photos of the twins, and both of their names spelt out in letter magnets. Every surface of the house seemed to have disappeared under piles of books and toys, and Becka looked tired but happy. Earlier, she'd outlined their busy weekly schedule – toddler playgroups, social worker visits, play therapy, baby sensory, forest school and online music class. 'I'm busier now than I've ever been at work!' she'd laughed. Her enthusiasm and energy to attend so many groups and educational experiences with the boys, to provide as many positive experiences for them as they could, impressed Alice straightaway.

But Alice couldn't help but feel a pang of jealousy as she witnessed how easily, how naturally, Becka inhabited this new role of 'Mum'. Watching her moving around the kitchen tending so lovingly, so intuitively to the needs of her little boys, chatting casually to Alice, Alice envied her friend and her relaxed approach to motherhood while Alice still felt so awkward, so unsure, so wracked with insecurities about the journey ahead.

Alice hadn't heard from Adrian or Michael lately, which was unusual as Michael was one of the most active posters in their WhatsApp group, often recommending a book or podcast that he thought the other adopters may be interested in. Adrian was the king of the funny meme, a staunch supporter of the prep group participants, and always the first to congratulate every milestone of each of their journeys with a smiley face or supportive message. She hoped they were doing okay with their newly placed son. The last they'd heard from either of them was Adrian's message to the group a few weeks before. He'd mentioned they were struggling a little bit with attachment and bonding: *'But it's early days, and I'm sure things will get better with lots of time and lots of love!'*

He'd sounded cheerful and upbeat, but Alice couldn't help worrying about the new family. She hoped they were getting all of the support they needed to settle in these early days.

She agreed with Becka that she'd drop a message to the group later to check-in for any updates, hoping that might encourage the new dads to contact them if they needed to chat.

Armed with heavy mugs full of coffee and a plate each of Becka's mother-in-law's amazing homemade coffee and walnut cake, Becka and Alice moved into the lounge. Becka quickly settled the twins to play with their collection of toy cars and fire engines and sat down to enjoy a morning of catching up.

Charlie popped in from time to time, waving to Alice and kissing the boys' heads as they played, but made the most of the opportunity to catch up on washing and sorting out the twins' clothes.

'So,' Becka smiled. 'Introductions start on Monday! How're you feeling?'

Introductions was the name for the period of time, usually two weeks, when the new adoptive parents spent an increasing amount of time with their new child, first at the foster carer's home and then at their own. It was a carefully planned process, designed to allow the child to gradually transfer their affections and attachment from the foster carer to the new parents at the child's pace. The introductions phase had clearly gone really well for Charlie, Becka and the twins, judging by the contented way the twins responded to their new mums.

Alice took a long sip of coffee as she chatted to Becka about all the complicated emotions filling her head around the exciting weeks ahead. She watched the twin boys now playing happily on the mat in front of her, listening to their giggles and chatter. This was the kind of mum meet-up she'd always hoped to have, meeting up for coffee and cake while the children played happily, and Alice tried to imagine what her days would soon be like with her new little five-year-old companion. She wondered if Tegan would get on well with the other adopters' children, if she'd do well at school, what she'd like to do at the weekends, and what her hobbies would turn out to be. The prospect of becoming a parent overnight to a child who was already so fully formed in many ways was quite overwhelming for her at times. This was a young person who'd experienced so much life before coming to live with Alice and George and Alice had spent the previous night in and out of sleep, bothered by anxious dreams as the date of introductions loomed closer.

What if she didn't like them or didn't settle well? she thought. What if we can't help her, and what if, after all this time and training, we still haven't done enough?

Alice

NOW

It hadn't been an easy journey to approval, Alice mused the next day as she sat in front of her computer, ordering last minute items for the child who was about to arrive in their home. She remembered the many meetings she and George had had to complete with their assessing social workers in order to prepare for panel. The most challenging of those meetings had been the individual assessments.

Alice remembered how she had curled up on the sofa with a cup of tea, taking small sips as she mentally prepared herself to delve into her past while Cara, the assessing social worker, had settled into the armchair opposite, pen in hand.

They were about to begin the individual assessment, which was a vital part of Alice and George's adoption home-study. Cara explained that previously, prospective adoptive couples were interviewed together. However, after instances where domestic violence had been uncovered between the applicants, safeguarding measures were tightened. From then on, partners were interviewed individually to avoid such abuses being hidden.

'All fine!', George had smiled after his interview – an efficient, thirty-minute run-through of his life – the week before. And now it was Alice's turn. She knew for her, it wouldn't be quite so simple. Cara's kindly face turned to her and smiled.

'Shall we begin?'

Nerves began to tumble in Alice's stomach as she began to describe her childhood, a happy, simple time with loving parents, a close-knit gang of friends and memories of playing outside in the summer. Bikes, skipping ropes, and warm, freckled skin all featured heavily in her memories of that time. Her mum, standing at the sink, smiling at her children as they devoured freshly baked cakes at the kitchen table after school. Alice thought it had been a perfect childhood and dreamed of recreating it with a child of her own.

School and university had passed without issues. Alice related her academic achievements, the friendships she'd made, graduating with her parents standing proudly, one at each side of her, huge grins filling their faces.

Cara smiled now as she made copious notes, but then, her pen came to a stop. Alice's words dried up, and the mug of tea in her hands went cold. A sense of dread pooled in her chest as she got closer to describing the most difficult time in her life so far.

She watched the story of her life unravel, like a movie-goer who can't look away, and her heart lurched as sun-dappled images of her childhood left the screen. What replaced them was the dark, shadowy backdrop of a horror story, as memories of her relationship with Axel pushed their way forward, needing to be told. Cara's expression was patient, now, as Alice's voice faltered and cracked.

'I just need some water,' she said as she jumped up and ran to the kitchen. Alice knew she had no choice but to be honest with her social worker, but she wanted to delay the moment all the same.

It had all been so thrilling in the beginning. Twenty-two years old and fresh out of university, Alice had started a part-time job in a bar to supplement the income from her daytime admin job. It had been exciting to find herself the object of the charming, dark-haired bar manager's attention. Axel was charismatic, popular, ready with a shared joke for every punter, and had a friend in every bar they visited.

When Alice first started working behind the bar, he'd surprised her by noticing her straight away. Axel would wink every time she walked by, and would stop any conversation he was having to ask Alice how her evening was going. His laser-focus gaze made it feel as though he really wanted to know. And so Alice, being unused to such attention, glowed in his spotlight.

Axel didn't believe in mobile phones, so he was never distracted. When he spoke to you, his whole attention was on you and nothing else. It was intense and unnerving, but thrilling. Alice flushed red in the wake of his charisma, curious to find out what was causing the sardonic smile that always played at the side of his mouth. She spent many evenings trying to work out what was going on in his head, questioning the choice of music he put on behind the bar, or the off-hand comments he made as they worked alongside each other. It was fair to say that Alice became infatuated with him, and Axel knew it. Many pretty girls drank in the bar and flirted with him all night, but he wanted to spend his time with Alice. And she couldn't work out why.

'You know you remind me of a firefly,' Axel said, bestowing the nickname upon her one evening. It was dark outside, and he'd just rang the heavy bell at the side of the bar to call time, winking at her, signalling that it was time for their end-of-shift gin and tonic and a debrief of the evening. An intimate time, with the lights low, and the deserted bar heavy with silence as the night fell outside. A treasured time for Alice as her stomach bubbled with nervous anticipation of the much yearned-for connection with this man who made her feel a mix of passionate emotions and excitement that she'd never experienced before.

Alice tightened her ponytail anxiously and waited expectantly, remaining quiet as she and Axel waited for two old men to drain their glasses and leave. She watched impatiently, willing them to move as they heaved themselves up slowly from the leather armchairs by the fire, slapped each other on the back and headed for the door.

'Night, gents,' Axel called while flipping a placemat carelessly between his fingers. He was lazy, relaxed and had all the time in the world, and Alice wanted nothing but his undivided attention. She'd waited her whole shift with anticipation bubbling in her stomach, and the fizz of attraction making her hungry for his gaze. Smiling at customers, pouring drinks, wiping down counters, all the time buzzing with the chemistry that grew inside her, knowing his eyes were watching her across the bar. Every move she made felt highly charged, with his attention trained only on her.

Now, she poured their drinks, ice cubes clinking noisily in the silence of the now empty bar, and sat down opposite him, knowing that Axel always waited until he had Alice's full attention to speak, never before.

'Fireflies are known,' he said, his gaze heavy with meaning, 'for their conspicuous use of bioluminescence during twilight to attract mates or prey. So, as I'm now hypnotised by the light in your eyes, which one am I? A mate, or prey? Tell me, firefly.' He demanded, draining his drink, never breaking an almost painfully intense eye contact with dark eyes that were pools of lust, dragging Alice, powerless, into their depths.

And from that moment, she was hooked, never to recover.

Becka

THEN

Picking up the post on the way up the stairs, Becka let herself in and made space on the coffee table for the pile of bills, flyers and takeaway menus she found piled up against the door. The metal coffee table was cluttered with tattered copies of a lesbian lifestyle magazine, overflowing ashtrays, half-empty cans of lager and takeaway cartons, and the dust in the room twinkled in the air as the midday sun flooded the room. Misty, Luna's pet cat, curled her tail around Becka's legs, yowling insistently for food as Becka reached down to stroke her soft, grey head.

Luna, Becka's girlfriend, had a loft apartment that might be considered trendy, but it could do with a thorough clean, Becka thought, as she pulled up the blinds and cranked open the huge windows to let in some fresh air.

Not even stirring at the light, Luna was asleep, stretched out and fully dressed, on the leather sofa against the wall of the open-plan living space. A talk show played on the TV, left on from the night before. Becka sighed at the familiar sight and took off her shoes, padding quietly to the kitchen to brew some coffee. It was midday, and she needed to get back to work on a commission piece that she'd promised to deliver to a client by the following day, but she had something she wanted to say to Luna first, and it couldn't wait.

It had been some party the night before. Luna was the popular lead singer of an up-and-coming local rock band, and she and Becka had spent the night in a small, sweaty pub in Camden with about fifty other people Becka hardly knew, celebrating the launch of the band's new album. Always the extrovert, and a minor lesbian icon in their circles, Luna loved these kinds of events, chatting, drinking, smoking and partying into the small hours. Becka wasn't quite so keen, the novelty of attending these things on Luna's arm had worn off quite early on, and now she'd like a night in from time to time. Not that she'd tell Luna that.

Becka had left the overcrowded pub at around 2 a.m., leaving Luna with a drink in one hand and her other arm around the shoulders of a pretty young fan who Becka recognised as Eve, a regular at Luna's shows (and most of the after-show parties too). Too jaded to be jealous, and too tired to care, Becka had pulled her jacket over her head against the rain and ran to the nearest taxi rank to get home, where she collapsed thankfully into bed with a cup of tea and two paracetamols, determined to start work at a reasonable time the following day.

'How's Eve?' she said without any actual malice, as she saw Luna stretching and stirring on the sofa, pulling herself into a sitting position at the smell of coffee.

'Oh, hey babe, I'll have one of those if you're making one. Thanks, chick. Didn't hear you come in. Quite a night last night, huh?!' Luna laughed, running a hand through her short spiky hair, dark eyeliner smudged under her eyes. She came up to Becka in the galley kitchen to pull her into a hug.

'You know Eve's not a patch on you, gorgeous. What time did you head off?'

Luna yawned as Becka finished making the coffees, and they sat cross-legged across from each other on the kitchen bench. Becka knew that what Luna really wanted to do was drink coffee, smoke cigarettes and dissect the evening before. Who wore what, who was with whom, who'd argued with whom… the usual routine that Luna enjoyed so much on these occasions. They'd chat and laugh, then head to the café downstairs for a greasy all-day breakfast. Becka knew the usual drill, but today she was steering the conversation in a different direction, she didn't have time for a lengthy breakdown of the party today.

'So, Luna, have you thought about what we talked about last night?' Becka started, knowing she wasn't going to get a positive response from her half-asleep, hungover girlfriend on this one, but needing an answer all the same.

The two women had met on a night out a year before, via mutual friends. Luna had just gone through a messy break-up, and Becka had initially steered very clear. Still, there was something about the way they always ended up at a bar together at the end of the night, telling ridiculous jokes, doing shots, not wanting to go home and always finding their way back to each other that made her wonder if Luna was worth taking a chance on. Becka was a sucker for a confident girl, and Luna wore her sparkly charisma so lightly, so easily, that Becka was quickly enchanted by her, despite her cautious nature when it came to women. In the end, they went home together and somehow didn't end up parting again. For a while they'd been the golden couple. The ones everyone wanted to see at a party and talk to at the bar and Becka had been proud of her gorgeous girlfriend who, when she sang, made her feel like the only girl in the room.

Not long after, Becka realised that she and Luna had grown up living just streets apart. Back then, Luna S was Lana Smith, two years ahead of Becka at school. Lana had left behind the brown pigtails, school uniform, and the stammer she had tried to hide, when she left school and transformed herself into Luna, with spiky black hair, tattoos on both arms, and an attitude to match.

Lana and Becka were never friends, but Luna and Becks were a pairing who couldn't stay away from each other. At school, Becka had been ashamed of her sexuality, embarrassed and awkward after coming out shyly to a friend who had snubbed her ever after. She never quite found her confidence in relationships after that. But meeting Luna changed everything.

Being gay and in love with Luna was like nothing she'd ever experienced before. Having felt awkward for most of her teenage years, Becka blossomed in confidence in Luna's orbit. Luna made her feel alive, sexy, passionate and proud of loving girls. Imbued with the thrill of being Luna's girlfriend, Becka cut her hair short, dyed it purple and blue and got her first tattoo. As Luna's girlfriend, being gay went from being a shameful secret to being the most incredible source of pride.

'You're bloody gorgeous, you know that?' Luna would whisper, breathily, in her ear as she pulled Becka close, her breath smelling of whisky and cigarettes after her shows every night. Ignoring the jealous looks of the girls in the front row, Becka kissed her girlfriend sensuously, running her hands through Luna's hair and feeling like the luckiest girl alive. Beautiful Luna, in her leather jacket and black eyeliner, always the star of the show. If only those who snubbed me at school could see me now, thought Becka. Successful artist, gorgeous musician girlfriend, happy to be gay. How things have changed.

But their relationship, if you could call it that, had stayed light ever since and Becka had had enough. What no one knew about the golden couple was that Becka would swap it all for a cosy night in. Late nights, parties, lazy hungover days, a flexible approach to monogamy, cigarettes, and alcohol were all very well for a while. But living the party girl life had begun to wear thin, and Becka wanted to know where she stood.

'Babe, don't start all this again. Not now, will you?' Luna complained, tapping the cigarette packet on the table to release her first smoke of the day and wandering over to the open kitchen window with it, perching on the wide windowsill. Becka sipped her black coffee – which she hated, but there was never any fresh milk at Luna's place unless she brought it with her – and considered her next move. It was no good, this relationship was going nowhere, and they both knew it. Becka also knew that Luna wouldn't be the one to end it.

'Luna, we've been together for a while now and every time I talk to you about being more serious with each other, about what may or may not be going on with Eve, about moving in together, you avoid the question. And I'm tired of it, I just need an answer.'

Luna had been Becka's first love, she knew that now. Their relationship was feisty, passionate and exciting. Luna, impossible to pin down, always up for an adventure, never wanting to settle down, had caught Becka's heart and turned it upside down. Their arguments were explosive, and the making up was even more so.

Tenderly, Becka looked at her lover now, silhouetted in the morning light, tendrils of smoke curling up into the air around her. Her eyes traced the tattoos on her bare arms, up to the soft, shaved hair that she loved to stroke at the back of her neck. Becka loved everything about Luna, she adored her as much as she had done the first time they met. But she knew it was time to say goodbye.

As if reading her mind, Luna looked at her and smiled, the wide smile that melted Becka's heart every time, forgiving Luna every transgression under the sun.

'You want it all, babe.' Luna said. 'Becks, you want the home, the marriage, the babies, the traditional shebang. And I don't. You know that life's not for me. It never has been, never will be.' She paused. 'I love you, Becks. But this is me. This is my life and that's not going to change just cos I'm turning thirty. But you will and that's okay. It's been fun, hasn't it?!'

Becka walked up to Luna, and sat on her knee, kissing her girlfriend for the last time. 'You brought me to life, you know,' she said quietly.

'And I've never loved anyone as much as you, chick. You know that,' Luna replied, squeezing Becka's bum as she spoke, incapable of ever being too serious.

But Becka knew it was true. Luna might flirt with every girl she met, but Becka knew her heart belonged with her. But it wasn't enough anymore. It was time for them to go their separate ways, knowing they'd never forget what they had.

Holding each other tight, the two women hugged and kissed goodbye, and Becka stroked the back of Luna's spiky head tenderly for the last time. Inhaling the smell of her at her neck, she kissed Luna's cheek.

'Be good,' she whispered.

'Ha! As if!' Luna laughed in response.

Becka smiled as she ran lightly down the stairs of the apartment building, towards a new life, without Luna in it. It had been fun while it lasted, but she knew it was never meant to last long. That much was clear now. A starter relationship, she thought. And what a start it had been. Now it was time to open the door to a new life in which, just six months later, she'd meet Charlie. A contented relationship that very soon would set them both on the path to marriage and motherhood, and the life Becka had always dreamed of.

Alice

NOW

Her mother had always told her to steer clear of men who badmouthed their previous girlfriends. It was never a sign of a healthy relationship, she had said. Alice didn't understand what she meant at the time, but she did now.

Following another draining and emotional session with Cara, Alice had grabbed her coat and fled the house, desperately needing a change of scene. Now, she stirred her coffee mindlessly with a spoon, hoping to drown out her own thoughts amongst the constant buzz and chatter of the café. Still, the monologue inside her head only got more persistent as her brain struggled to process and sort out her memories of the past.

The city centre café was small, noisy, and bustling, nestled in the corner of a busy shopping street. It was popular with the passing-through commuter crowd picking up their coffees before heading off to work. Not the kind of local café where the staff knew your name and your coffee order, there was complete anonymity. It was a place where you could sit nursing the same coffee for an hour in the corner without anyone bothering you for conversation, which was exactly what Alice was looking for. So she shrank into her seat in a booth at the back, pulled her cardigan tightly around herself, warming her hands on her mug.

It had been a tough session today. Cara had encouraged Alice to dig deep into her memories of life with Axel. She'd spoken more honestly about that time in her life than she'd ever done before. She felt vulnerable as her emotions were stripped bare.

Bit by bit, Cara had helped her to process the frightening memories she had of the final day she'd spent with Axel, the defining moment of their relationship. The turning point that had pushed her to flee and left her feeling tainted and dirty inside. Bringing those memories into the crisp air of this beautiful winter morning felt wrong, and she was struggling as the memories, freshly released, swirled hauntingly around her head.

THEN

'It's what you deserve, you useless, untidy, dirty, waste of space…'

Insults had flown freely from Axel's mouth, and the viciousness of his words had echoed tauntingly inside Alice's head that day, as the pain had slowly begun to subside. It made no difference that he was now at work, and she was left in the quiet. The house was clean, tidy, and calm, after she'd spent the early morning, as she always did, rising silently and painfully out of bed before he woke, ensuring it was so. His imposing self could very well still have been hovering, threateningly behind her. Looking over her shoulder, whispering endlessly in her ear, breathing down her neck. Alice always heard his voice criticising everything she did, every action she took, every thought she had. A nameless, creeping fear shadowed her every movement these days.

That morning, Alice stood very still. Afraid to move, afraid to jolt her aching, sore body. She held herself as though she would break into pieces if she moved too fast. Standing in front of the bathroom mirror, she tentatively held a cold, damp flannel to the angry, purple bruise forming around her swollen eye.

She barely recognised her pale, beaten reflection. Her eyes looked empty, shadowed by dark circles, and her hair fell lankly to her shoulders. Her head ached, and the blushing of her cheeks had merged with the hues of her bruises as she recalled the events of the night before, and she was suddenly covered in an ugly emotion resembling shame.

Axel had begun raging at her after arriving home late, drunk and angry, again. His temper was inflamed by the dirty frying pan sitting by the sink, which had been left to soak and was to be washed in the morning by Alice, who'd gone to bed early with a headache after a long day at work.

'What the fuck is this, fire-fucking-fly? We don't live in a fuckin' squat.'

Dragged out of a fitful sleep by Axel spitting abuse at her and violently pulling her out of bed by her arm, Alice fell roughly to the floor. Then Axel threw one drunken punch, his fist connecting with Alice's cheekbone, before he collapsed in a drunken stupor on the bed. Shuffling away, not daring to make a noise, she crept as quietly as she could to the spare room before he could wake again.

'I love him,' she whispered quietly to her reflection, her voice breaking.

Looking back on this night, she will wonder what madness had befallen her, to make her believe that what she was experiencing had anything to do with love.

'No, I thought I loved him,' she corrected, her voice becoming stronger as tears had started to fall. Alice slid down the wall to the cold bathroom floor, heart-rending sobs shaking her whole body, never wanting to know heartbreak like this again.

Peggy

NOW

Peggy mopped the kitchen floor for the second time that day, humming under her breath as her mid-morning classic tunes radio show played in the background. It was a beautiful crisp autumn day outside, with the birds singing cheerfully in the trees and the sun shining brightly through the kitchen windows and bouncing off the shiny countertops. With the children at school and the morning jobs done, Peggy was getting ready for her second cup of coffee of the day. Looking around the small, neat kitchen, she felt satisfied that the house was prepared for the social worker visit she was expecting at 11:00 a.m., so she tidied away the mop and bucket in the tall kitchen cupboard, and flicked the kettle on to boil. Tegan had been grumpy, loud and difficult to motivate that morning, slopping the milk from her cereal on the way to the sink. She'd loudly protested going to school that day, and her tardiness meant they'd had to rush out of the door to get there in time. The sticky floor had had to wait until Peggy got back from the school run to be cleaned.

Peggy was an experienced foster carer who had looked after many children on both short- and long-term placements throughout her thirty-year career. During that time, she thought she had seen the whole range of behaviours, from the often highly traumatised children in her care. Strict routine, clear boundaries, nurture and low-pressure days made up the recipe for success that Peggy had used favourably with children from two to eighteen years of age. Known lovingly as 'Gramma' to her kids – both her own kids and the foster kids she cared for – she always had a pack of tissues and sweets in her handbag, and lots of hugs for the children who needed them.

Over the years, Peggy had learned to be reliable and diplomatic in her dealings with the social care teams she worked with. She knew when to bite her tongue, even if she disagreed with how the child's care plan was made. She worked with a positive, compliant mindset with the teams who decided what was best for these children. And although Peggy fretted about whether contact arrangements with birth families didn't seem to work well for the child, she trusted them to make the right decisions for the children in the end, even if it didn't always feel right at the time.

However, this time, Peggy felt strongly that she needed to speak out when she saw Sami that day. She was concerned that the adoption plan that had been decided for Tegan really wasn't right for the child. She knew she couldn't keep quiet over something that she felt could have devastating consequences for the child and the adopters with such high hopes for their new family.

Sami had a lovely relationship with Tegan. During her visits, Tegan was generally upbeat and positive, playing with Lego and chatting with Sami happily about the prospect of a new home and new family. Sami saw the best in Tegan, which warmed Peggy's heart, and she was truly good at her job. She had a genuine affection for the children she worked with and was driven to obtain the best outcome for every child in care that she had on her caseload. However, Peggy was concerned that in this particular case, Sami's apparent soft spot for Tegan was preventing her from seeing the realities of the situation. Adoption was not suitable for this child.

Tegan loved her birth mum, she lived for contact with her and had an immense loyalty and sense of responsibility towards her. She wasn't going to let go of her first mummy and embrace a new mummy and daddy that easily, no matter what she said to Sami. Worried for the hopeful adoptive parents and the potential impact on their whole family, Peggy became anxious. She popped the kettle on and waited for the doorbell to let her know that Sami had arrived. Much had to be discussed before introductions with Tegan's new parents started the following day, and Peggy sincerely hoped that it would all work out for the best.

Alice

NOW

The day had finally arrived – it was the first day of introductions. The day they'd meet their long-awaited daughter for the very first time.

It was a bright, sunny morning, and Alice jumped out of bed, feeling like it was Christmas. She hadn't slept a wink and George had been up since 6:00 a.m., cleaning and organising the kitchen, bringing her up a coffee in bed half an hour before, planting a soft kiss on her forehead and whispering, 'Good morning, Mummy'. Alice believed she couldn't have been happier than she felt at that moment. Nesting was kicking in for both of them, and they were so excited for what the next few weeks, and the rest of their lives, as a new family would hold. Alice had texted Becka the night before, deliberating over what to wear and getting hung up on small details, despite Becka's reassurances that she just needed to be herself, be relaxed and enjoy it.

A text buzzed on Alice's phone now: 'Have a great day! Will be thinking of you all. I can't wait to see some photos! Lots of love, Mum xx'

The day before, Becka and Charlie had popped by with the twins to catch up over coffee. They gave some last-minute moral support and advice as they'd all sat together in the garden watching the twins race around on the lawn. George had looked so natural with them as he'd chatted gently to the boys, offering them a drink and a snack. Alice had felt so proud that this amazing man she loved was about to become a father. They had finally completed the lengthy assessment process together to get this far in finding their family.

And now it was time to meet their girl. Alice and George got into the car, far too early, and their first stop was the introductions planning meeting. Stopping off for a coffee on the way, they sat in the car and looked at each other, barely knowing what to say, the adrenaline and nerves of the day building for them both. Alice's stomach was swirling with anxiety, and her hands became clammy and cold. She was sure she could hear her heart racing in her chest. They were the first in the meeting room at the social services offices despite their efforts to disguise their promptness by lingering over their coffees and visiting the bathrooms after they arrived.

Whilst they both understood the vital importance of this meeting in planning a smooth transition for them and their new child, they couldn't help looking at the clock. They wished the time away as they waited for the meeting to end so that they could head over to the foster carer's house to spend the first few hours with their daughter. They had waited so long and done so much preparation for this moment, and now it was here. They didn't want to waste one minute on practicalities when they could be spending time getting to know the newest member of their family.

They'd both been delighted when the foster carer had sent them a video of Tegan via WhatsApp the night before, as she had grinned and waved at the camera and shouted, 'Hello Mummy and Daddy! I can't wait to meet you!' while cuddling the fluffy green dinosaur that they had sent her as a transition toy. They struggled to focus on everything that was being said during the prep meeting. It was a blur as they answered questions with dry, nervous mouths, and then finally, the moment came. Everyone got up, shook hands and packed away their files. It was time for them to meet their child, at last.

Arriving at the foster carer's house, Alice's throat suddenly became dryer than ever.

She gripped George's hand tightly and knocked on the door. This is the moment my life is about to change forever, she thought. Everything felt as though it was happening in a blur as the door in front of her opened. George made polite conversation with the foster carer, who was lovely and kind and had done so much for Tegan to settle her over the last year. Then all of a sudden, Alice saw a small girl racing down the hall and running towards her, throwing herself heavily against Alice in a huge hug, grinning at her and shouting 'Mummy!'. As she returned the warm hug and dropped to her knees to say hello properly, Alice thought to herself – this is what I've been waiting for. This is what I've been working for all this time. This is who I am. I am mum.

She allowed herself to be pulled by the hand into the living room and fell to the floor to play. She submitted to a cuddle attack from a tickly dinosaur toy, brandished by a whirlwind of a small child, and loved every minute.

The following two weeks were fun but exhausting for the new family. Every day, their social worker called to check in and see how introductions were going. And on the fifth day, when Alice, George and Tegan were tired and full of cold, she said, 'Yep, no adopter I've ever known has survived introductions without getting a cold at some point! It's par for the course. Take care of yourselves, get early nights and enjoy this time as much as you can!'

Over the two weeks, they spent their days in the park, in soft play centres, driving around in the car singing nursery rhymes and Disney tunes at the top of their voices. They ate packed lunches in the car, walked the dog through the woods, and watched children's films at the foster carer's house, while cuddling under blankets on the sofa with popcorn. They did crafts, painting, colouring, played endless games of catch in the garden and drew pictures together. The first time they went out by themselves with Tegan, flying solo as new parents, they'd visited a soft play centre. After which, Alice and George had both collapsed in a tired heap on the sofa, worn out after trying to keep up with their energetic five-year-old all morning. Her chatter was incessant, and her energy levels seemingly insatiable. She didn't sit down for long and was full of beans. Alice put it down to the excitement of the new start. She took a photo of their shoes together on the floor next to their table at one point to post proudly to Instagram with the caption: *'First day flying solo as Mummy and Daddy and loving it!'*

During the two weeks, they learned a lot about themselves and about each other as their different abilities as parents began to emerge. George excelled at the morning routine, waking Tegan up in the morning and chivvying her along to get dressed for the day with the good humour, playfulness and patience that Alice had admired in him from the day she met him. While Alice spent her days chatting to Peggy whenever she could, alongside caring for Tegan. She was desperate to learn as much as possible about the girl's routine, her likes and dislikes, and how she was getting on at school. She felt she had this limited time to catch up on the first few years of her new daughter's life before she was on her own as a new mum. Pages of her notebook were filled with information about her new dependent in her neat, small handwriting over the space of the two weeks.

Every day they spent together was one day closer to becoming a family, and the prospect daunted and excited her in equal measure. She had to get this right.

Adrian

NOW

Taped to the door was a word-processed paper sign, flapping in the wind and loosely protected from the elements by a torn plastic wallet.

'Stay and play, every Tuesday, 10 a.m. – 12 noon. Tea, coffee and a biscuit = 50p. All are welcome!'.

Eager to get out of the rain, Adrian nervously pushed the heavy church door and stepped inside the busy hall. He held his son tightly by the hand as the little boy agitated to be set free. Adrian had no idea why he was so nervous – this was a toddler playgroup and he's used to chairing high-level meetings at work every week, for goodness' sake! – but he couldn't shake the feeling and started to wish he'd stayed at home with Joey this morning. At least there, he knew that there was no one to see him when Joey had a meltdown. Adrian's confidence in parenting started to wobble. Scanning the room, he could quickly see that he was the only dad there and, he guessed, the only adopter. Although, of course, he couldn't be sure of that. Some days he felt as though he walked around with a sign on his head, proclaiming his newness as a parent. Joey was three years old, but Adrian was just over four months into parenting and on days like today, he felt that more than ever. Thank goodness he'd arranged to meet Becka and the twins here for some moral support, or he was sure he'd have turned around and be heading back to the car by now. He then ran through the checklist that was constantly going through his head these days – Joey had slept well last night, he's had a drink and snack in the car, and he's in a clean nappy. That should allow Adrian some time to catch up with his friend while Joey played, he thought.

'Come on, Daddy. Come ON!' Joey was imploring him now, his attention caught by the array of plastic toys in the corner of the room. Adrian spotted Becka, looking flushed, heading back from the ladies' toilets. She had a twin in each hand, and a bag slung over her arm that looked packed for a weekend away.

'Hi, sorry, sorry, double nappy changing emergency!' she laughed. 'Have you been here long? We'd been here about five minutes when these two BOTH decided it was the perfect time to poop! Typical, eh? I'm ready for a sit-down and one of this church's finest mild roast coffees. How about you?!'

Adrian had finally texted Becka back that week after a challenging day with Joey. They'd agreed to meet up with the boys so that the children could get to know each other and they could share stories of parenting so far. He was finding opening up about the challenges they were facing difficult, so Adrian had been relieved when Becka had spent the evening texting him back and forth, providing advice when appropriate, as well as some much-needed perspective and understanding.

The two parents moved over to the toddler area that was ring-fenced by crash mats. Adrian suppressed a smile at this. Had they known his son was coming today? He and Becka settled the boys with a selection of toys and sat down at a table to watch the three children play. Adrian kept an eye on Joey, interested to see how he'd react to the two smaller boys and was ready to step in to encourage him to play nicely if needed.

'What I find so tricky is when I talk to other parents, and they tell me "oh yeah, my three-year-old does that too!"' he confided to his friend now. 'And it's so difficult to explain the differences. Yeah, all three-year-olds have tantrums and meltdowns, I know that, but the trauma that we see in him, the intensity of it, it's just next level.

'I guess I just find that, well, other parents don't really understand because they've seen their toddler have a tantrum, so they think it's that… but it's just not. It's a whole world of difference, but I can't find the words when I try and explain it.'

'I get it,' Becka replied, cradling her coffee in both hands. She looked like she needed it. 'It's not the same. Not at all. This is some next-level parenting! When our kids are in meltdown, they're in fight or flight, maybe they're in regression, perhaps it's an unmet need from their past that they're communicating to us. Then you throw in attachment difficulties and sensory challenges too, and that's a whole new world to learn about. And we get to figure that out, but you know, we're just finding our way in the dark with this. It's tough. There's no doubt about it.'

There was so much that Adrian wanted to say. So much he wished he could talk about and get some reassurance on. He stopped himself, for fear of oversharing or dominating the conversation. If he could have done, he would have talked about the times he'd been hit in the face, punched, scratched, kicked and rejected. The meltdowns he thought he'd never be able to calm, the inconsolable crying, the way his child pulled away from him when he tried to comfort him. The feeling of not succeeding as a parent in the way he'd hoped he would. The feeling of never being able to make up for the experiences this tiny boy had had before they met him, and the fear they never could.

Many other adoptive parents talked about feeling a rush of love for their child in the same way you would for a baby born to you. And Adrian understood how love could grow – he felt so much protectiveness and affection for his little boy that he was sure could grow into love with time. But sometimes, when he read about others proclaiming to feel that way, it made him feel small, inadequate, and as if he was doing something wrong. Adrian mused, if only they'd talked more about just how complicated the emotions can be post-adoption in their prep group training. There was so much focus on how the children might be feeling – and rightly so – but no real mention of the rollercoaster of emotion a new adoptive parent might feel. But, instead of saying this, he stood up, offering to get fresh coffees as the first ones had, unsurprisingly, gone cold after many interruptions from stampeding boys. Once settled with coffees and biscuits, with their children happily building a tower with bouncy bricks, Adrian and Becka fell naturally into easier conversational ground – parental anecdotes and a general catch up.

'So,' Adrian smiled wryly. 'I normally leave Joey to eat his lunch in the playroom while I potter in and out and do jobs because, well, toddlers. But that day, I'd decided that we'd sit and eat together, an opportunity to connect, you know?! So, I'd just started eating, and I looked up. That moment, he looked me in the eye, opened his mouth, and slowly regurgitated half-eaten spaghetti bolognese back onto his plate. Oh my god, it was savage! Ha-ha, my stomach just turned!'

He paused to dramatically put his hand over his mouth and fake heave while Becka spluttered on her coffee, her shoulders shaking with laughter, and her eyes dancing with mirth.

'That wasn't even the worst part! He picked up his fork and went to pick it back up to eat it again. Oh my, if that wasn't the foulest thing I've ever seen in my life! Never again!'

'Oh wow, toddlers are savage!' Becka was properly giggling now. 'You just have to laugh, don't you? Or some days, well, I'd be rocking in a corner, crying by 9 a.m.!'

The friends regale each other with anecdotes, funny moments, light-hearted re-tellings of tricky parenting moments from the previous few weeks. Laughing about the screaming, crying, push-pull of parenting children from a complicated past as a shared survival strategy. Helping each other find the humour in those moments that sometimes felt impossible to manage. Somehow, out in the light of day, with strong coffee, a good friend and lots of laughter, it felt so much more manageable than it did in the dark, lonely times at home. At last, they started to tidy up and gather the children.

'Can you imagine,' Adrian grinned as he piled their coffee cups onto the trolley in the corner of the room. 'If they ever let us two give a talk at an adoption training event? No one would ever adopt again! No sleep, regressions, food issues, headbutting, biting, and more!'

'Ha! Where do I sign up?!' Becka laughed wryly as she wrangled two wriggly and reluctant toddlers into splash suits and wellies. 'We love them, really!'

Sami

NOW

Despite her ever-increasing workload, and the toppling paper mountain on her desk, Sami loved facilitating the local authority's adoption preparation courses – or 'prep group', as it had come to be known.

It was one of her favourite parts of the job. It was so easy to become disillusioned as a social worker, to become demoralised by the seemingly endless stream of negativity that working in child protection could bring. Prep group, on the other hand, was overwhelmingly positive. Yes, they informed new adopters of how difficult it could be, the challenges they may face. But it was a time for couples or individuals to become new parents, and become a family, when they might not have had the chance otherwise. And that, in Sami's eyes, was always something worth celebrating.

She'd been particularly proud of the guest speakers she'd found to present during the most recent training events. Not long before the event took place, she'd managed to get in contact with an adult adoptee, her birth mum, and her adoptive mum. They were a perfect choice to speak at the training event. They'd overcome challenges, trauma and complicated life-story work until they'd become a robust and united family, twenty years after the daughter's adoption. They all got along so well that positive contact was encouraged between all three members of the triangle.

The (now professional, working in childcare) daughter, Emma, had spoken engagingly with eloquence, wit and pride about the journey she'd been on. She expressed gratitude for the work her adoptive parents had done with her and the challenges she'd faced as an adolescent coming to terms with her past, and her life story. She became emotional when talking of the joy she felt when her mother had helped her contact her birth mother once she'd turned eighteen. The room had fallen silent as she'd started to speak, and there wasn't a dry eye in the room amongst the prospective adopters or trainers once she'd finished. Sami had felt a rush of pride and sheer joy inside her at that moment, reigniting her love for the job that she was able to do and the families she could help to form. Looking around the room and seeing how the talk had motivated the adopters, she felt the inspired energy in the room. Animated conversations broke out as soon as they stopped for coffee and Sami was confident that she'd done the right thing bringing Emma and her family in to talk to them.

But she also knew that not all adoption stories had such a hopeful ending. She was not naive enough to imagine that all stories would turn out so happily, but focusing on those that did helped her avoid the cynicism and negativity that threatened to overwhelm her on difficult days. Particularly on days when her own past pain was triggered as it so often could be in this job.

Sami pushed the thought away briskly, that was long in the past now. It hadn't happened for a long while and it wouldn't happen again, she wouldn't let it.

Alice

NOW

The night before they were due to bring their daughter home for good, Alice and George were tired from fourteen days of introductions, early mornings, late nights and overwhelming emotions. They'd spent many hours in the car, shuttling back and forth, to and from the foster carer's house for soft play and day trips. Exhaustion had crept into their bones. They'd been living on strong coffee, chocolate and quick meals they could pop in the microwave for two weeks now. All of this on top of an underlying vibration of stress – the stress of trying to be perfect. The immense amount of effort they put in ran through every day as they attempted to charm this little girl, for whom they wanted to be the whole world.

They were shattered but determined to make the most of their last evening as a childless couple. They rented a film and popped the cork on a cold bottle of fizzy Prosecco, ordering in their favourite Chinese food. As they waited, they chatted with tired, lazy voices. Trying not to fall asleep in the soporific warmth of the fire that crackling hypnotically in the grate. Yearning to be nurtured, Alice changed into soft, cosy pyjamas and bed socks. She cuddled up next to her husband on the sofa and tried to calm the frenetic racing of her mind.

Before the takeaway arrived, George went to the kitchen to mix drinks – gin, tonic, and lemon, a favourite of theirs for celebrations. While he was gone, Alice happened to look up at the television, and her attention was abruptly grabbed by the heart-wrenching cry of a child. It was an advert for a children's charity and the combination of sad images, suffering children and emotive music tugged painfully at Alice's heartstrings. Suddenly, all in a rush, she felt an involuntary convulsion of emotion explode from her chest. Then she was crying, big, gulping, noisy sobs that shook her body from the inside out, and she couldn't stop, tears rushing down her cheeks.

'Hey, what is it? What's the matter? Hey, what can I do?' George was by her side, holding her hand, the warmth of his body encouraging her to fall into his arms. Yet the tears kept on coming. All the emotion, the grief, the years of trying that had brought them to this moment. It was all pouring out and could no longer be contained. Everything they'd hoped for, everything they'd tried, all the ways their lives were now going to change. She held on tight to her husband, her rock in every storm, and just let herself feel it all as he pulled her close.

Piper

NOW

Across town, Sami was running late. Again. Parking abruptly up on the kerb, making a cursory check for parking restrictions, she threw open the driver's side door impatiently. 'Fuck', she swore under her breath as the hem of her trouser caught on her heel. She pulled to loosen it and stumbled hastily out of her car. It was cold, icy and rainy. Sami could see Piper waiting anxiously and shivering up ahead. The other woman was dressed in a light coat despite the freezing rain, twisting her handbag's cord nervously between her hands.

What kind of incompetent social worker kept a pregnant woman waiting on the street in this weather? Sami berated herself firmly. She shrugged her heavy winter coat, with scarf already threaded through the arms, quickly onto her shoulders. Sami grabbed her umbrella from the boot and walked as quickly as she could, slipping, sliding and dodging the icy patches underfoot. She waved and mouthed a 'sorry, sorry!' as she moved closer to Piper. This needed to go well. Sami didn't want to put the other woman off at this early stage or threaten the carefully established trust they'd recently managed to form between them.

The two women had come to view the part-furnished housing association flat that Sami had been able to arrange for Piper to move into, now that she was expecting a new baby. Since having Tegan removed from her care at the age of three, Piper had worked with social services, finally accepting their support, to turn her life around.

Demonstrating a strength of character and resilience that Sami had seen in very few birth parents, Piper had pulled herself back up from the rock bottom she'd found herself painfully hitting. Extracting herself from an abusive relationship that she'd fallen into when young and vulnerable, Piper had slept on a friend's sofa until she'd managed to get herself back on her feet.

Attending every contact session with Tegan until the girl was adopted, Piper kept in contact with social services, accessed support services, got clean and gave up alcohol and cigarettes. She'd also found, and kept, a part-time job in a corner shop. Sami had visited the shop on a few occasions over recent months while Piper had been working. It had warmed her heart to see how much the job and the support of a good manager and colleagues had helped boost Piper's fragile self-esteem.

For many of the women Sami worked with, raising self-esteem was vital to stop them from repeating the same mistakes and re-entering the same unhealthy relationships they'd found themselves in before. Statistics showed that many birth mothers were care-leavers themselves, meaning that they had few parental figures to guide them once they reached adulthood, often confusing cycles of abuse with love and care.

It was hard to break these generational cycles, particularly in that community, Sami reflected. She thought about the boarded-up houses, and evidence of unemployment and drug dealers working in broad daylight, that she'd often seen when she'd visited Piper and Tegan in their former home together.

It was a weight off her shoulders knowing that both mother and daughter would now be safe, away from the dangers that had marred their early years together. They would be protected in their new homes.

Sami breathed a sigh of relief as she greeted Piper with a smile, leading the way up to the front door of the apartment complex. Moving day wouldn't be far away now, and feeling the mother-daughter case coming gradually to a close, Sami felt a satisfying sense of a job well done.

Peggy

NOW

It was moving day for Tegan. The sun was shining, the birds were singing, and the frost was crisp on the ground outside. Everyone in the household was up early and excited, ready for a mini party and warm send-off for the youngest member of their little family.

Peggy had spent the evening before baking and icing a special cake and decorating the small living room with balloons and streamers. She did the same whenever any of her children moved on. She battled now with conflicting emotions of her own sense of loss mixed in with excitement for Tegan as she gazed upon the cheerful red and yellow 'congratulations!' bunting in the window.

Peggy's two lively pre-teen foster sons had been up since 6:00 a.m., squabbling loudly and fighting over glue sticks and felt-tips. By some miracle, they had succeeded in making a sticky card that wished Tegan 'Gud look' in her new home. It was now standing proudly on the messy kitchen table.

'Do you think she'll like it, Gramma?' the eldest had asked, uncharacteristically shy, at breakfast time.

'She'll love it, pet.' Peggy had squeezed him in a quick hug and dropped a kiss on his bed-flattened hair.

As for Tegan herself, she was crashing around in her bedroom, chatting loudly to her stuffed toys about the day ahead. She was happy to be moving and had spent the previous day yelling sporadically at Peggy about the whereabouts of her special things, making sure everything had been safely packed before she left. She'd been talking about nothing but how amazing life with her new family was going to be for days on end.

Peggy silently worried about how her new placement was going to go but kept her fears to herself. She'd expressed these fears early on to Sami, Tegan's placement social worker, but Sami hadn't shared her concerns. And now the match was finalised, introductions had been completed, and today Alice and George would be arriving at 1 p.m. to take Tegan back home with them.

It wasn't that introductions hadn't gone well, they had. Peggy liked Alice and George, and the two weeks had gone relatively smoothly. Tegan had been lively, happy, engaging and entertaining. She'd looked forward to the exciting activities her new parents had planned for her and skipped out of the door with them every morning. She seemed to bond immediately with her new adopters who saw nothing but the funny, happy, charming little girl she could be. Tegan had returned every afternoon full of tales of fun about all of the ice creams, her new toys, her new rainbow-themed bedroom and the walks with her new dog.

Peggy loved seeing her so happy, but at the same time, she reflected sadly on the unsettled evenings she'd had with Tegan after the new parents had gone home. That was when the mask slipped, and all the anxiety and fear the little girl had been holding in all day would come out. Peggy had been a foster carer long enough to know all about the 'honeymoon period' when a child meets new adopters. She worried that what Alice and George thought was a sign of them bonding and forming a solid attachment to Tegan – whom she called Mummy and Daddy from day one – was a false calm that came about due to the little girl's survival instinct kicking in. She was masking and putting up a front. Presenting as an amenable, charming, happy little girl so that they would love her and not reject her as she'd already been rejected. Only Peggy knew just how much stress and anxiety was bubbling under the surface of that perfect mask, and how difficult it would be for Tegan to keep it up for much longer.

Peggy had tried to do her best to prepare Tegan for adoption. She had a real soft spot for this little girl, greatly admiring her character, spirit, and resilience after such a tough start in life. Despite the admiration Peggy held for her, she knew that the girl could be challenging.

Peggy was warm-hearted, kind, strong, firm and fair. She was loving with all of her foster children and highly experienced in caring for traumatised children. She knew that when a child said to her, 'I could hurt you. I wish you were dead forever' that they didn't mean it. All it meant was that they were hurting inside. Still, it was different for adoptive parents to understand that, particularly at first. They'd invested so much in being great parents to these kids, and they didn't have the professional distance a foster carer could have. Peggy loved these kids, but she also knew she was doing a job, whereas adopters want a family. They want to give and receive love and affection, and that's not easy with these kids.

Peggy wanted to prepare Tegan as much as she could to ease the transition to her new family. In the little study, where the children liked to watch DVDs, was a bookcase full of child-friendly books about adoption. She'd sat down with Tegan every evening after dinner over the last few months and read books to her, explaining what a new family meant.

Though, like many five-year-old girls, Tegan struggled to understand the realities of adoption. She'd had her emotional goodbye contact with her birth family a few weeks before. Still, Peggy didn't think that it had really sunk in for Tegan that she wouldn't be seeing them again once she was adopted. Peggy knew from experience that once the novelty of a new family had worn off and the reality of everyday life set in, with its usual rules and expectations, Tegan would start to struggle. The grief and loss would set in, and that's when the challenges would begin for the new family.

Peggy just hoped quietly, as she carefully ironed the last of Tegan's clothes to pack, that they'd be strong enough to withstand the inevitable storm that would ensue. She still didn't fully believe that Tegan's adoption plan was right for the child (or the new parents, for that matter). It had seemed to Peggy that reunification with her birth family could have been a possibility at one point. Still, it wasn't Peggy's place to question the children's plans. All she could do was love and support them as much as she could while they were in her care, and prepare them as much as she was able to for their next steps.

In the life-appreciation meeting that took place just a few weeks before, Tegan's class teacher (a kind, young woman) had gushed tearfully about what a fairy tale ending this was for Tegan. Peggy had sat, her voluminous handbag on her lap and the bruises from Tegan's last trauma-fuelled meltdown on her wrists, and kept quiet. She'd bitten her tongue, knowing that the teacher had only the best of intentions, yet had worried every day and night. Instead of selling the fairy tale to these adopters, the professionals in charge of Tegan's case would have been much better off sitting the new parents down and speaking honestly about the very real challenges they were about to face. Peggy knew that none of the difficulties Tegan presented were her own fault. She was just an innocent, frightened and traumatised child, after all. Why would she trust adults when they'd never done anything but let her down? Peggy knew all about the long-lasting impacts of early childhood trauma, but she loved all the children in her care, no matter what challenges they brought with them. Still, she was also realistic about what made up a successful adoption. Presenting an inaccurate picture of Tegan's challenges was doing nothing but setting the new family up to fail.

Alice

NOW

'Good morning, hot Mumma!' George whistled as Alice appeared at the top of the stairs, grinning. She came downstairs and gave him a twirl, dressed in one of her favourite full-skirted red vintage dresses, with her curly red hair pulled up into a bouncy, high ponytail. These were her happy clothes. Laughing, she let George grab her gently around the waist and swing her into his arms, kissing her glossy red lips.

'It's finally here!' she smiled, laying her head on her husband's shoulder and breathing in the smell of him that she loved so much – the clean, woody scent of his aftershave. 'We're going to be parents,' she whispered. 'You're going to be the best dad there is!'

After the exhaustion of introductions, it had been blissful the night before to soak in a long, deep bubble bath and pamper herself a little. She'd also chosen and laid out the outfit she'd wear today. Alice had wanted to mark this day; it was the biggest day of their lives. She was ready for photographs that she knew she'd treasure forever, and she was feeling fabulous. Introductions had gone so well and she couldn't wait to get to know her new daughter. It felt like a new era of their lives was about to begin.

Today was placement day, as the introduction plan called it – 'new family day' as Alice and George thought of it. They both knew that this would be a difficult day for Tegan and were ready to tackle that together. But nothing could dampen the excitement they both felt at finally becoming parents. Their house was full of flowers and cards from well-wishing family and friends, and Tegan's bedroom was decorated and full of new clothes and toys. They were ready.

'Hey, it's a gorgeous day. It's cold out there, but it's sunny,' George called to his wife as she plumped up the cushions on the sofa for the hundredth time that day. 'It's meant to be nice all morning, and the house has been cleaned to within an inch of its life, and we've nothing to do. We don't want to sit around twiddling our thumbs all morning getting stressed, so why not go out?'

'Sounds like a great idea, lovely. Let's go and enjoy the day. It'll be a while before we have the chance to spend time just the two of us again!'

Picking up their favourite takeaway coffees on the way, they drove out to one of their favourite country parks with the dog for a blustery, sunny walk. They loved getting outdoors and going on long walks with their dog, then returning home tired and ready to curl up in front of the fire, particularly at this time of year. They walked and chatted, then sitting down to feed the ducks and geese with the mix of birdseed and bread brought with them, they heard shouts and giggles of children playing in the park on the other side of the lake. Instead of the spikes of sadness and jealousy that such sounds would normally incite in Alice, she felt nothing but contented happiness this time. She knew that very soon she'd be bringing her own child to play in that same park.

Alice and George enjoyed the rest of the morning in each other's company. They ate an early sandwich lunch in the little café just outside the park before heading home to drop off the dog in time to get to Peggy's house for 1 p.m.

The day started well. Anxious for it to go smoothly, Alice and George followed the placement plan to the letter. They'd packed and moved the majority of Tegan's belongings during the second week of introductions so that all they had to bring on placement day was the child's overnight bag. This was designed to make the emotional moment of final goodbyes with the foster family as easy as it could possibly be on the day. Alice and George had been told to keep it short, not accept cups of tea, and ensure goodbyes were brief (they had given Peggy lots of hugs, flowers, and a thank you card the day before). Now, loaded up into the car and pulling away from the foster carer's house, Alice felt a strange mix of emotions. She couldn't quite believe that she was bringing home her daughter for good. They had a child in the back of the car, dressed in a superhero cape, clasping a rag doll, staring out of the window, coming to live with them. Alice couldn't even begin to imagine what she must be thinking and feeling. A fully grown, walking, talking, thinking child who'd exhausted them over the last two weeks of introductions already. Who knew what full-time parenting would bring?

As pick-up had taken place in the early afternoon and they hadn't wanted to go straight home, the new family headed for a local petting zoo. Tegan was bubbly and excited, running from one enclosure to the next, shouting 'Mummy, Daddy, look!', grabbing their hands and swinging off their arms. She was full of beans. It was strange to think that this was their first proper day as a little family of three. Alice looked around, thinking that anyone walking past would see them being just like any other family. Catching a glimpse of her reflection in a window, she startled slightly at how she looked like just another mum. She carried a 'mum bag' full of snacks, wet wipes, water bottles and toys. And she had a small girl pulling insistently at her clothes. A girl who called her Mummy.

But in her head, a nagging voice told her she was a fake, that someone would come along any minute and tell her to give this child back. Despite these feelings, Alice smiled wide and tried to enjoy every moment of being called Mummy, meeting the needs of this child she'd always wanted. George took lots of photographs and they both held their girl's hand whenever they could, enjoying the opportunity to show her around and talk to her about the animals they saw.

Once they got into the car to go home, Tegan was tired and became quieter. It was 3:30 p.m. when they got home, and they walked up to the front door together, Tegan grabbing George's hand tightly.

'Here we are! Home sweet home!' George smiled as he put the key in the lock, his hand gently on Tegan's shoulder. Alice and George shared a tired, loving smile which faded slightly in surprise as they heard a muttered 'Home STUPID Home' from the small girl by their side. Her little face flushed brightly as they both looked at her mildly, choosing not to respond. Alice's vision of taking a smiley doorstep photo of the three of them on Tegan's first day home faded.

Once inside, Alice and George decided it was time for some cosy cuddles on the sofa and a film to wind down after a big and exciting day. First, Alice took her daughter upstairs, excited to put away some of Tegan's possessions in her new bedroom. Together.

'Come on, lovely, let's go and put some of your things in your bedroom!' She smiled encouragingly at Tegan, not expecting the response she received.

'Why should I?' came the answer. But Tegan followed her upstairs. It wasn't quite the bonding moment Alice had hoped for, but it was better than nothing.

Once upstairs, Alice laid out a cosy onesie for Tegan on her bed – it was a dinosaur with multicoloured spikes on its back. Perfect for this feisty, spirited little girl. Smiling, Alice took Tegan's hand, leading her into the lovely new room they'd spent so long putting together.

During visits to their home in introductions, Tegan had run into the room declaring everything 'amazing!' and 'beautiful' and 'just what I've always wanted!'

But now, Tegan pulled her hand away, became sullen, ran and jumped under the bedcovers, refusing to wear the new onesie and put her arms tightly around herself. It was as if she feared they were going to rip her clothes from her.

Sami had told them that Tegan loved dinosaurs and Alice had wanted to get everything right for her. Now she felt strangely hurt by Tegan's adverse reaction. It was as if she'd done something really wrong as a mum already, but she couldn't figure out what it was.

Feeling helpless, Alice sat gently on the edge of Tegan's bed, placing a hand on her daughter's small shoulder. Not understanding what had just happened, she could only hope that time and patience would somehow break through the wall of fear that had suddenly sprung up between them, and her new daughter would learn to trust her, one day at a time.

Adrian

NOW

'Maybe you hold him at arm's length,' the support worker suggested.

Indignant, Adrian didn't know what she meant. He cared for Joey, played with him, kept him safe, and worked hard every day to meet his needs. Irritated at what he read as criticism, he felt himself shutting down at her words.

Swirling red wine around his glass later that day as Michael prepared dinner, he communicated this irritation to his husband, only to find it growing when his husband agreed with her.

'Yeah, I know what she means. I don't think she means it in a bad way, just that, well, you could get closer to him sometimes.'

It had been an initial telephone conversation with the adoption support worker to assess their need for play therapy. Adrian had explained, proudly, his daily schedule of activities for his son, only to be met with a light-hearted pushback from the woman on the other end of the phone.

'Don't be afraid to get messy with him,' she said. 'Not everything has to be perfectly organised and scheduled. Get down on the floor, laugh with him, let him climb all over you, tickle, kiss and wrestle him. It will build attachments! Let him play with his food, drink from a baby bottle, go back to weaning, squashing banana between his fingers. Finger paint each other! Remember, he's never done this before. These are all the things he's missed out, and he needs them now, with you!'

The Adrian of five years ago would have been appalled at this. Still, now the idea of such messiness was anathema to Adrian as he looked around his clean, tidy home. But attachment was the aim, and he knew he needed to try something new if this was to work.

Things had been tricky, and so early on in placement, it was hard to find the headspace to ask for what they needed. Still, after many long conversations with Michael, Adrian finally put in a painfully honest telephone call to Sami. He spoke openly about the struggles they were experiencing in attaching to their new son.

Joey's arrival threw them so much it felt as though all of the pieces of their former lives were up in the air. New parenthood became their new lives, their job, their everything. They circled, exhausted and hyper-vigilant, around this small, angry boy and his needs, as though monitoring a volatile bomb that could go off at any time. Cuddles and rewards were few, and tears were plentiful (not only from the child). They lurched from one meltdown to the next.

Their lives seemed unrecognisable. Adrian often felt an indescribable discomfort at how their neat, organised lives had become so dominated by this messy, unpredictable child.

After Joey was asleep, they often collapsed on the sofa with takeaways and chocolates, rather than the restaurant-inspired meals Michael had always loved to cook. Too tired to do anything much, even talk to one another, they zoned out in front of the television until one or both of them fell asleep on the sofa.

Some nights, Michael spent the evening in his study lesson planning, while Adrian read books on parenting, trying desperately to find some way of breaking through the seemingly impenetrable wall of trauma that surrounded their new son.

Now Michael looked at his husband, teasing him. 'Come on, I know you hate mess and like structure, but give it a go! You never know, you might enjoy it!'

'And anyway, it's just one child,' Michael winked. 'Think of me leading thirty year 2 kids in arts and crafts on a windy day – now that's chaotic!'

Adrian shuddered but laughed, agreeing to give it a go. It might be messy, it might push Adrian to his limits, but if this play therapy worked, they were willing to give it a try.

Alice

NOW

Bundled up in layers under her winter coat, Alice blew on her cold, numb hands and fidgeted from one foot to the other as she waited. Had it really been seven hours already since she'd dropped Tegan off this morning at 8:30 a.m.? The day had seemed to disappear. The house was clean and tidy, order had been restored to Tegan's bedroom and playroom, and Alice had spent the afternoon completing an online training course on therapeutic parenting, dashing out the door when she realised it was 3:15 p.m. already. Wishing she'd brought a comforting, hot coffee in one of her colourful reusable cups, Alice sighed. Taking care of her own needs seemed to have fallen to the bottom of her list of priorities lately. Anxiously, she fingered the snacks she'd brought for Tegan in her pocket as well as the fidget toy she'd been advised to keep on hand. It was an attempt to quell the after-school restraint collapse meltdowns that had marked every day of that week so far.

She hoped that today might be different.

Alice stood awkwardly on the edge of the chattering group of parents huddled expectantly outside the bright, yellow door, unsure how to become part of this already established community. She fixed what she hoped was an approachable expression on her face and kept her gaze on the door of the reception class. Tegan had been attending for just a few weeks, and it hadn't been an easy time. Alice willed the class teacher to appear. Her skin prickled as discomfort ran up and down her spine. Was she imagining it, or were the other parents avoiding looking in her direction? Steering their children quickly away from her and Tegan like she was sure she'd seen them doing yesterday at pick up? Were they turning away from her when her well-intended attempts at engaging them in conversation had ended up being stunted, awkward and brief?

Alice, George and Tegan had been cocooned at home as a family for most of the last half term, trying to build attachments before Tegan started at her new school. 'Snuggling in' was what Tegan had adorably called it the first time her social worker had come to visit. It was common practice for adopted school-age children to be kept off school for a while, to allow them to settle and feel safe in their new home, but Alice had worried about Tegan missing out on opportunities to learn and make new friends, something she'd already missed out on so much before coming to live with them.

George had gone back to work, and Alice had been excited to start this new stage of her life as a 'school mum' and not least because she was physically aching for some time by herself after the intensity of the last few weeks. Tegan's anxious chatter and need to be near them at all times, to know what they were doing, when, how, and why, was entirely understandable but also exhausting. Alice yearned for five minutes of her day where she could sit quietly and enjoy some calm. She longed for the school day's predictable routine and the structure it would bring to all of their lives. Walking around the brightly-coloured corridors of the primary school during Tegan's settling in visit, the familiar smell of PE kits, dinners and disinfectant, brought back happy memories of her own school days. Alice listened to the head teacher as she told her about pastoral help, nurture groups, and emotional support sessions, and had thought that, with this school's help, they could do this. Together.

That had been just three weeks ago, and Alice had been called into school several times since. Tegan was struggling to settle, and Alice felt at a loss as to how to help her.

She'd sat in meetings with the head teacher, the ELSA (Emotional Literacy Support Assistant) TA, Tegan's class teacher, and her social worker, and had felt anxious and impotent every time. She was called into these meetings where they asked for her opinion and looked to her for guidance. At times she felt overwhelmed to such an extent in her mind that she felt like exploding. As though she should shout 'I'm not her mum!' to all these people, and imagine the shock that would cover their faces. She then felt a flood of guilt and shame that this thought had even crossed her mind.

Suddenly becoming a mum to a five-year-old overnight, expected to instinctively know and understand what they needed, felt like an impossible pressure. Every day, Alice felt like an imposter.

She felt like she was looking for someone else to help her parent this child she didn't know, but the only parents she had now were her and George, and they were floundering in the dark.

Every time Alice looked around her house now, she found it hard to recognise herself in her new life. There were splotchy paintings on the wall, a school uniform drying on the radiators, and small shoes and coats on brightly coloured pegs at the front door. Barbies sat and stared with expressionless faces at her while she took her ten-minute-long baths in the evenings. She washed small clothes covered with paint, felt tip pen marks and dirt every day.

From the school newsletter pinned on the corkboard to the mumsnet weekly emails she received on her phone, everything about her life told her that she was now a mum. It was everywhere she looked. But why then, in the midst of this new identity, didn't she feel like one? Why did it feel as though she was babysitting someone else's child? When would it start to feel real, and when would she begin to feel like this – incredible, brave, resilient – child was hers?

'Mrs Armstrong?' It took a few minutes to realise that the kind class teacher was talking to her. Holding Tegan by the hand, the friendly reception leader had her hand gently on Alice's arm. Alice felt a slightly nauseating alarm at how much this simple gesture made her want to cry. Gathering herself quickly, she painted on a quick smile.

'Yes, sorry, I was miles away! Hi, thanks – Tegan! How are you? How was your day, lovely?

'Mrs Armstrong, could we just have a quick chat? You look frozen! Come in. Miss Jones, our class TA, she can make you a drink – tea, coffee? And she can watch Tegan while we have a chat.'

Settling Tegan into the neighbouring classroom with a colouring book and the listening ear of a friendly TA as she chatted about her day, Alice sat down on a tiny chair across from Mrs Weaver. As the hot steam and comforting odour of the milky coffee hit her senses, a mantra started up in Alice's head – please, just don't ask me if I'm okay. Don't ask me, please. She didn't trust herself to not reveal every thought she'd ever had if this lovely woman asked her anything like that. This is not a confessional, she firmly reminded herself, biting her lip painfully as she forced herself to focus on the teacher's account of Tegan's day.

'We've had some complaints from other parents.' Mrs Weaver paused, her voice quiet. 'I didn't want to worry you and George over it. I know it must be difficult, so early on. We're all trying to support as much as we can in school, but after the first few, I thought it best to inform you. You know, so we can see if we can work together on this?'

The familiar feeling of helplessness came over Alice, bubbling anxiously underneath the outwardly capable persona she was working so hard on presenting. She'd read so much, completed so many training courses and watched so many documentaries, but when it came down to it, addressing the issue of her daughter's violent outbursts and the lashing out at her peers felt beyond her. Talking for a while to the kindly teacher about possible solutions brought little relief. So, she took Tegan by the hand and despondently headed home. Alice knew she must put away her pride and call honestly upon the prep group's support that evening.

On the way home, Alice turned up the radio and, with a cheer she didn't quite feel, encouraged Tegan to sing along with her as she drove. Belting out the words to a pop song she knew, Alice's mood lifted when she heard the cautious sound of her daughter starting to join in. At that moment, no melody could have been more beautiful.

And slowly but surely, the magic of music spun its web, creating gossamer threads of connection as mother and daughter sang out loud, collapsing into giggles when they didn't know the words. Feeling upbeat by the time they got home, Alice grabbed Tegan's tiny hand and held it tight.

Fearing the good mood between them could dissipate at any moment, Alice soaked up the moment of connection, smiling kindly at the small girl by her side. She wished for these precious, fragile moments to last. But for now, the new life with her daughter felt constructed of such delicate glass, prone to breakage at the slightest of knocks.

Adrian

NOW

It was precisely 11:12 a.m. when Adrian pushed open the heavy door of the dark wood furnished coffee shop. He hungrily ordered a large double-shot gingerbread latte, a grilled cheese sandwich and the biggest double chocolate muffin in the shop. Twelve minutes had already passed, all too quickly, since he'd dropped a sticky-fingered Joey off. It was the little boy's first lunchtime settling-in session at his new nursery, which meant three hours of child-free time for Adrian. He tried not to outwardly express any impatience as he waited for the noise of the milk steamer to subside. Adrian couldn't help feeling that parent-alone-time passed at twice the speed than it did when you were awoken at 6:00 a.m. by a small boy poking his fingers into the corners of your heavy, still-asleep eyes.

The drop off had been strangely easy. Adrian had been expecting tears or at least a small sign of reluctance from the little boy. But Joey had simply waved quietly and walked straight in, obediently holding the hand of the nursery worker who'd greeted them at the door. Adrian had stood still for a moment, feeling a strange mix of emotions – was this normal? Was this a sign of attachment issues? Was his little boy okay? Should he be leaving him? But before allowing the parent guilt to set in, he'd returned to his car, which felt strangely quiet (though still filled, as it now always was, with crisp crumbs, food wrappers and small, muddy footprints). Removing the nursery rhyme CD and turning the radio up loud for once, he'd headed to the coffee shop just out of town.

Michael had texted him that morning: *'Enjoy your few hours of freedom today, gorgeous! Wish I could be there spending it with you! x'*. That was the downside of having a teacher as a partner. If Michael had any other job, Adrian would have pushed him to take a few hours off to make the most of this opportunity to spend time together as a couple. But as that wasn't possible for teachers in term-time, Adrian had brought a book to the café and looked forward to drinking his coffee and reading without interruptions for a couple of hours.

Seated at a table in a homely corner by the wood-burner, Adrian unwrapped his soft, cashmere scarves and placed his warm, woollen winter coat over the back of the chair. He took a sip of his coffee and breathed in deeply. A child cried, loudly, suddenly, at the other side of the café, and Adrian jolted, looking around. Adrian imagined, now that he was a parent, that he would begin to experience the same sort of instinctive reaction that made breastfeeding mothers involuntarily lactate when they heard a baby's sobs. He was a parent now. It would ever be this way.

The child was settled by their parents, and Adrian breathed deeply, gazing into the hypnotic red and orange tones of the crackling fire. This quiet time to sit back and reflect was simply invaluable at this stage of his parenting journey. So much of the time, he felt he was getting it all so wrong. He was exhausted, lurching from one meltdown to another, and his ability to parent Joey intentionally – as he desperately wanted to – was so often compromised by the amygdala-hijacking screams that often started before they'd arisen from their beds. Itchy clothes, lost comfort blankets, and too-shiny sunlight were all enough to press down hard on their son's sensory sensitivities. They set off his internal alarm bells, manifesting in urgent, ear-splitting screams for help. By 9:00 a.m. most mornings, Adrian already wished they could start the day all over again.

But today, he felt a glimmer of hope beginning to seep into their lives, and he was keen to share the progress they'd made with the rest of the prep group. Opening up the WhatsApp group they'd formed to keep each other updated, he started to type, smiling as he read the last message in the group, which was from Charlie: *'Oh my WORD. I love these two terrors with absolutely everything I have, but bedtime and gin can't come quick enough today! #terribletwos'.* This was accompanied by crying and poop emojis, as well as a picture of a living room so filled with toys and snack plates that the floor was virtually unable to be seen. Adrian knew from their text chats that Becka had spent the Saturday before at her sister's, helping to look after her baby niece as the family had moved house. Charlie had clearly had a day of it with the twins in her wife's absence.

Adrian wanted to update the group on the Attachment play therapy work that he'd been doing with Joey. Despite his initial defensiveness towards the support worker, he knew that Attachment play therapy was an evidence-based approach that helped attachments in young children and their adopters, so he reluctantly gave it a try.

After the mixed feelings brought on by the assessment call, Adrian was encouraged when the cheerful adoption support worker arrived a few days later with a bag full of toys, cotton wool balls, crayons, plain paper and balloons filled with glitter.

She showed him how to make a dedicated play space by throwing a blanket over the carpet and placing cushions around the edge for them to sit on, with toys in the middle. Joey had been difficult to engage at first as the excitement of a visitor and new toys sent him into an over-stimulated state of manic play, resulting in him hitting Adrian several times in the face.

Julie, the worker, had gently guided Adrian into using playful approaches to redirect his over-excited son into playing nicely, taking direction from his dad. It wasn't entirely successful, but Julie pointed out that the idea wasn't that Joey was fully compliant in all of the games they initiated, but that Adrian and Joey learned ways to connect that they could use at other times.

There were a few moments during the session when Joey looked at Adrian and giggled adorably, tiny hands clasped trustingly in Adrian's larger ones, and Adrian started to understand how this approach might help them. And after the tricky start they'd had, that meant the world.

He thought of Alice and George and the difficulties they'd hinted at in one or two of their last messages. He wondered whether Attachment play therapy might be the answer for them and their new daughter too?

Adrian felt optimistic for the first time in a long time. Lulled into contentment by the warmth of the fire, the coffee, the food and the solitude to think. He was keen to share what they'd discovered with his prep group friends.

It had been tough, but Adrian and Michael's lives had gradually begun to shift and mould around the new member of their family. And now they both felt that a tiny glimpse of light was beginning to break through which, to them, was everything.

Becka

NOW

It was early morning, and the whole day was stretched ahead of them, with the winter sun streaming in through the big, slightly grubby, sash windows. The house was cosy, as the smell of buttered toast and fresh coffee lingered in the kitchen. A soft warmth emanated from the fire crackling in the hearth, gently heating the cold air inside the high-ceilinged Victorian townhouse.

How she loved their home, Becka thought, remembering the day she and Charlie had arrived to view the house for the first time.

THEN

They stood on the doorstep, nervously squeezing each other's hands, hoping it would be the one.

Becka knew her wife-to-be was an expert at narrowing down the perfect choice from many options, and Becka was one of those good choices. Theirs was the only date Charlie had been on after joining an online dating app. And as they ended up settling down together just a few months later, she had faith in her wife-to-be to pick their dream home.

They were planning their wedding and were so excited to find the perfect home to fill with kids and pets. And this house was perfect. Charlie could see it in Becka's joyful expression that she'd fallen in love straight away, loving everything about the beautiful home as they explored. Shiny, wooden floors in the second reception room (the playroom), the extended kitchen, the conservatory (a flagstone floored pantry!), and a magical, double-levelled garden with all sorts of nooks, crannies, and apple trees. It was the perfect home to raise a family.

They put in an offer and moved in during a heatwave just a few months later. 'Our dream home!' Becka cried happily as Charlie popped the champagne in the garden. She felt as though she couldn't be happier than she was at that moment.

Settling into their home as newlyweds was everything Becka dreamed of, immersing herself in making a home for her, Charlie and their future family. She pictured children running around the house and hearing their giggles, playing hide and seek, putting up a swing in the garden for them to play on. It was, to Becka, so beautiful.

Having moved into their dream home, they were now ready to begin the adoption process, and they wanted to start straight away, so Charlie arranged their first social worker visit. They tidied and organised the house to a standard of cleanliness that they knew would never be seen again.

On her initial visit, the social worker stepped across the house's threshold and exclaimed, 'Ooh, I like this house. It's so much nicer than your last one!' (she'd visited them previously when they were looking to find out more about adoption).

Becka and Charlie looked at each other, unsure how to respond. Charlie had been warned in advance not to make jokes while the social workers were around, and her jaw was already hurting from the fixed grin she'd pasted on since the moment the doorbell went. But she continued to say nothing and ushered the social worker in.

From that moment on, it was all go. They handed over all the paperwork they could for all the checks needed – driving licences, passports, council tax bills, insurance documents, car MOT statements, and any other paperwork they could find in a bid to be organised, committed adopters. They glanced through the health and safety checklist and made a tongue-in-cheek note to hide away their ceremonial swords before the next social worker descended upon them (if you're an adopter, you'll know, thought Becka, smiling).

Becka hid the gin, filled the fruit bowl, tacked paintings by nieces and nephews on the fridge, and developed a habit of walking around the house looking for toddler hazards. From then on, she glared at her wife whenever she so much as left a sharp knife out on the side after cooking.

Parenting preparation was in full swing.

NOW

Stepping gingerly over the scattered plastic toys underfoot, Becka, in fluffy pyjamas and slippers, ran through a mental checklist of the activities she'd planned for the day. Occupying her two little whirlwinds was a full-time job but for now, they were settled and comfortable on the sofa, drinking their morning milk, cosily tucked under a soft, white blanket. A few moments of calm.

Becka sipped her coffee, pushed her (ugh, so greasy) hair out of her eyes and looked over at her boys, smiling at the way they leant on each other. Their little legs in their feetie pyjamas stuck out from beneath the blanket, two sets of big blue eyes focused intently on Mr Tumble. It was moments like this where she had to pinch herself that they were here – a family.

She was a mum to two gorgeous, blond-haired, blue-eyed babies, and at times like this, she couldn't believe how fortunate they were that they found each other and became a family. She loved them so fiercely.

That was not to say it'd been easy, she mused. The sheer exhaustion she felt daily was something else. Trying to be the mum she'd always wanted to be was rewarding but tiring as she worked hard every day to give the children the experiences she wanted them to have – toddler groups, reading, playing, and giving them all the cuddles and affection that she could. All of her attention went on them as she tried to make up for everything they'd missed out on. It was so tiring, but so worth it.

On top of all of that, they had the continual visits, telephone calls, emails, paperwork, health appointments, and scrutiny from social workers that was like having an additional job as well as being an adoptive parent. Keeping on top of it all was certainly a challenge, and neither Becka nor Charlie prided themselves on their organisational skills but what they lacked in administrative organisation, they made up for in enthusiastic parenting. Becka loved the opportunity to be a child again, spending her days surrounded by colourful, noisy toys, and playing with her two little stars.

Becka and Charlie had never suffered from infertility. At least, they'd never tried to get pregnant. Coming to adoption as a first choice to build their family had been nothing but a positive experience for them and Becka was so thankful she'd never gone through the mental anguish of infertility, pregnancy, or baby loss. Now, looking at her two beautiful babies sitting so contentedly on the sofa in front of her, she couldn't imagine having built her family any other way. She loved being a mum, and being at home with her babies gave her a deep feeling of satisfaction that she'd never quite managed to find before. Becka smiled. This was everything she'd wished for – the beautiful home, her gorgeous babies, the marriage... Well, if she were honest, the marriage could do with a bit of work and attention right now, she'd be hard-pressed to remember the last time Charlie had referred to her as anything other than 'Mummy'. And as much as she loved hearing that, it would be nice to feel like a wife, or even better, like a woman once in a while.

She knew that she was so lucky, though – they were the lucky ones.

The boys were considered relatively easy in terms of adoption. Charlie and Becka had looked at each other and only just resisted rolling their eyes when they'd heard their babies described in that way. The social worker involved had meant that they (as far as they knew) were not affected by any of the issues that were so often found in adopted children. Children were so often affected by FASD (Foetal Alcohol Spectrum Disorder), severe developmental delay, or any significant neglect-related health side effects.

Whereas the boys had settled quickly, accepting Becka and Charlie as their new parents in a smooth transition. With her former social worker hat on, Charlie was always at pains to remind Becka that all adoption was trauma. Their boys were sure to experience attachment trauma and difficulties relating to this as they moved through their lives.

Becka knew this, she'd done a lot of research before adopting their boys, but she hoped that all the love they'd lavished on the children in these early days would only help make their lives easier as they grew. She hoped it would go some way towards helping them to heal from their difficult early life experiences.

The boys were still quiet now, sucking their thumbs, and entertained by the bright colours and singing flickering on the screen in front of them. So Becka allowed herself a couple of minutes to browse Instagram and scrolled to Alice's latest post. She knew that Alice and George had been struggling quite a bit in the early days of their daughter's placement. Still, the last time they'd spoken, Alice hadn't wanted to talk about it, so Becka had been stalking her Instagram daily to try and work out how things were going. It was hard to tell as all of Alice's posts had a positive spin on them. She clearly tried hard to understand and empathise with the painful journey of adjustment her new daughter was on. She'd put up a new post late last night, and Becka read it, full of admiration for the strength and resilience she'd witnessed in her friend since her new daughter had moved in:

'Our girl is incredible, and brave, and has survived so much in her short little life. But, of course, she has moments when she just needs to let it all out.' Alice had written under a picture of a shattered ornament that had been glued carefully back together. *'All the fear, all the feelings of pain, abandonment, lack of nurture, broken attachments, change and loss. It comes out in screaming, yelling, wailing, running around, tiring, exhausting, crying jags. These are not necessarily triggered by anything. At most, they are*

triggered by tiny moments, and the resulting wailing sessions seem, to me, to be entirely unrelated to the moment I thought we were experiencing. As the experts say, she falls into a room of trauma, stays there for a while, and then, if we're lucky, she climbs back out. At first, we didn't quite get this. We'd get drawn into it. But now we know better. I sit nearby with my coffee or a book, and I listen to the screams, the wails, and the incomprehensible "trauma chatter". I'm there so that when she's ready, she can come back to us. And she does. She goes into that room in her head, and then she comes back and often, not always, everything is calm and fine after the big feelings have been allowed to escape. They are heard, and they are out in the world. I like the phrase – when we know better, we do better. We know her better now, so we do better by her. We hold space for her enormous emotions, and we keep life calm, safe, and the same as it was when she left it. I found the emotional explosions very triggering at first. But now, not so much. I knew they weren't personal, but initially it was hard to see that. Now I can hold space for her whilst at the same time holding space for myself. We're learning together.'

Adrian

NOW

'I just don't know what's for the best. They're our friends, and I love them to bits, but at the same time, Joey's safety is what I care about the most. I feel terrible. I haven't got in touch since, and she hasn't either. It all feels so awkward.'

Adrian sat across from his husband, sipping a cold gin and tonic, watching the sunset. The evenings had just started to warm up, and after settling Joey to sleep, they'd lit one of the burners on their deck to sit outside and enjoy a drink together.

For the first time in ages, they'd left their son's room, held hands, shared a hug and smiled. There had definitely been a shift in how they'd felt as a family lately. The love was growing between the three of them, as if a heavy weight had lifted from their shoulders, replaced with the softest of baby blankets. Their hearts and minds felt light and full of love, it was almost as if they could see a glimpse of a happy future emerging from the relentless work of early parenthood. The night before, Joey had said, shyly 'Wuv oo too' for the first time when they'd kissed him goodnight and told him they loved him. It was time to celebrate, for sure. Adrian had chatted light-heartedly as Michael had busied himself pouring their drinks. Now, as they sat in the early evening light, listening to the calming sounds of the garden at night, it was time to chat about what had happened the weekend before.

'I know, I'm worried too,' Michael sighed. 'But to be honest, Joey's fine. He's fine.' Adrian looked over at Michael as he continued, 'I know, babe – I know it could have been much worse. But he's okay.'

'My main concern is for them, you know? It's clear that they're not coping, and I have no idea how to help them or what to advise.'

THE WEEKEND BEFORE

Adrian and Michael had wanted it to be a really special day. The first meet-up since they'd all had their children placed. What a milestone! It was an opportunity for them to celebrate becoming parents and for the children to get to know each other, play together, and they'd hoped, make lifelong friends. Adrian had sent out the WhatsApp group invitations and Michael spent ages planning the drinks, nibbles, and setting out toys for the children. When the day arrived, it was a sunny, bright day, warm enough to play outside.

They'd flung open the conservatory doors, put chairs outside and waited for their guests to arrive. The others burst into their home in a flurry of greetings, children and noise, offering a good bottle of wine (George), a pot plant (Charlie), and lots of hugs and kisses for everyone (Becka). Everyone delighted to be back together, but Alice hung back, quiet as the others caught up with excitement and joy bubbling in their voices. Hanging up the coats in the hall, Adrian spotted Alice dropping to her knees to address Tegan at the child's height, her voice carefully controlled and quiet, yet quivering with a fraught note of stress. Leaving them to it for a moment, Adrian crept away quietly to the garden.

Throughout the party, Alice was more withdrawn than the friends had all remembered her being before. At first, they'd put it down simply to the distracting nature of caring for children and assumed she'd relax once the children were settled and they could chat properly, yet Becka worried quietly to Charlie, remarking that every time Alice spoke, her voice sounded as though she were on the edge of tears, ready to spill out at any moment.

Settled in the garden with a drink and nibbles, children sitting on the deck with orange juices and biscuits, the prep group friends caught up, their words falling over each other's, fuelled with excitement, much as they had done the first time they'd met on their first training course, over a year before.

But the chat was different now, dominated by real-life stories of exhaustion, night-time wake-ups, toddler tantrums, and endless meetings with social workers. Talking was more difficult these days, punctuated with 'oh, sorry, hang on, wait a minute,' as they were interrupted by children and the endless parenting dance of snacks, cuddles, nappy changes, or simply entertainment when the children got tired of playing.

They were all seduced, lethargic and slightly giddy by the sunshine, the joy of seeing each other, the party atmosphere, and the peculiar emotional balm that came from sharing their experiences, imbuing them all with a happy sense of friendship and calm as children pottered happily around together, at times, clinging close to their new parents, at times, running wild in the large, verdant garden which was split level, meaning the adults could sit at the top, on the deck, while safely able to watch the children play on the grassy section below.

After playing football with the four little ones, Michael had just sat down – slightly red in the face and taking jibes from the group about his poor level of fitness, all the while blaming it on being a new dad and having no time for the gym – when Becka looked over to see Tegan take Joey by the hand and lead him into the playhouse.

'Look, everyone, how sweet – she's looking after him, bless her!', said Becka, unaware of the mounting anxiety on Alice's face and the way she went to jump out of her seat.

'Leave them, Alice, they're okay. They're just playing. Relax a minute, hey? They're just kids. I'll check on them in a minute.' George appealed to his wife as he got up from his seat, seeing Alice move to run over to where the children were playing. Reluctantly, Alice sat back down, but her face was pinched and tight, and she perched on the edge of the seat, every part of her body exuding anxiety. George dropped a kiss on her hair and headed off into the kitchen with Michael to make them both a drink.

Then it all happened so quickly. Tegan came out of the playhouse, but hadn't they just gone in a minute ago? And Joey was behind her, but his face was covered in tears. What had happened?

Adrian jumped up, 'What's the matter, Joey? What's happened?'

But his approach was too slow, everything in slow motion as Tegan shouted at the shocked adults.

'He won't do as I tell him! He's refusing to play my game and being STUPID! I don't want to be here. I hate this. I hate you all. I want to go home. You are not my Mummy and Daddy and never WILL BE!' The sad and angry little girl's voice escalated in volume as her tear-streaked face became redder and redder, pointing shakily at Alice and George in distress as she cried. Then she turned to run, dashing past and running into Joey, standing mute beside her, her speed toppling the small boy, shoving him until he tripped and toppled, falling face forward, down the stone steps. And time seemed to stand still as he fell in slow motion. The parents, shocked, rising up from their seats, Adrian racing to his small son, willing himself to catch him as he fell.

Everything seemed to happen in a blur. A brief silence as the small boy tumbled, then his screams filled the air.

All of a sudden, there was panic. Time slowed down and then sped up. And there was noise.

The anxiety in Adrian's raised voice clearly panicked Tegan, who ran to the bottom of the garden, screaming at the top of her voice, crying in distress at the panic she'd caused, not looking back as she ran at the flurry of activity she'd left behind.

And in the centre of the activity was a small child, scooped into his father's arms where, once safe, he screamed, and was comforted, held tight. Safe. Blood spilled from Joey's nose, mixing with his tears, the small boy startled by the pain and the shock of what had happened, but also from the explosion of noise and flurry of activity that it had produced. When picking him up, Adrian's heart leapt into his throat as he realised his little boy was coughing and spluttering as he spat out a handful of stones and dirt that he'd clearly been fed as 'dog food' during the game that went so wrong, mud, blood, snot and tears smeared across his red little face. Now all the adults were on high alert, gathering their children to them, heart rates elevated. Worried about what could have happened and shocked at how suddenly this lazy, sunny afternoon could have changed so dramatically. Charlie moved next to Alice, her hand on her arm as Alice stood frozen, unable to move or react, watching with a detached kind of horror unfolding on her face. George, seeing this, ran to the bottom of the garden to try to console a shrieking Tegan, who was huddled shaking in the shade of the big, oak tree.

It was hard to continue with the meet up after that. Once the initial flurry of activity died down, they calmed down the children, Adrian with Joey on his lap while the twins played near Charlie, who sat on a blanket on the grass with them, trying to bring some semblance of calm to an elevated mood that had unsettled everyone.

Tegan refused to come closer and sat with her back to everyone on the steps leading down to the lawn.

The conversation was awkward, stilted.

Alice shut down, and George's cheeks flushed with colour as he apologised profusely. The others tried to reassure and calm him, despite knowing their words were falling on deaf ears. It was clear that Alice and George wanted to leave and no longer felt comfortable with their friends. The party broke up shortly after, everyone hugging and promising to keep in touch. Alice was strangely silent and stiff as she held her child by the hand and walked out of the door.

Night was beginning to fall, and Adrian and Michael hugged their friends close, said their last goodbyes, shut the front door, and carried their sleepy little boy up to bed. They made sure to hold him extra tightly that night. Lots of extra cuddles and kisses were given, the three of them holding each other close until the little boy's long-lashed eyelids fell heavily over his big, brown eyes. He was soon fast asleep, tucked in cosy and warm under his dinosaur duvet, exhausted by the excitement of the day.

Awkwardly, the two dads had held a hushed but urgent conversation in the kitchen earlier while Charlie and Becka had played with Joey and the twins in the garden. They didn't want to upset Alice and George any more than they already were, but the concern for their son at that moment had been overwhelming. Ultimately, they decided that Joey was unharmed, just shocked, and that he would be fine. No rush to A&E was needed on this occasion. They looked at each other intensely, never had the sudden responsibility of new parenting hit them as hard as it did at that moment.

They sat back down in the garden, breathing in the fresh night air, the remnants of the party all around them. Taking a few minutes to de-stress and de-brief before tidying up. It was the sense of letting out a huge and heavy breath you didn't know you were holding in until then. The fairy lights that Michael had strung up in the trees twinkled as dusk fell around them.

Adrian tried to find the words to explain just how much of a rush of love and protectiveness he'd suddenly felt for his son at the moment he'd seen him put at risk. The instinct that had made him run to him, a feeling of utter urgency to protect this scared little boy who needed them so much. Michael reached for his hand, his firm grip telling Adrian that he felt the same way.

It had been a day of huge emotions. The happy, elevated mood of friends rejoicing in each other's company, laughing, sharing stories, chatting loudly and joyfully, that had turned so quickly to rush and panic and screams. Then a catching of the collective breath. A calming. A reassurance. Hushed words and things unsaid.

Tegan

THEN

I'm just going to stare out of the window until we get home.

I want to get home, have my dinner and play with my toys. I don't want to talk about what happened today. We were just playing. I don't know what all the fuss was about.

Adrian scared me by shouting at me and running up to grab Joey when we were in the middle of a game. That's why I cried and screamed so loud. It was all his fault.

And anyway, I don't care about them. I just want to be with *my* mummy. I'm so angry all the time because no one hears me, even when I shout really, really loud.

I want to see Mummy again. I want to live with her and to know she's okay. Why won't they tell me if she's okay and if she's found a nice place to live now too? A place with nice sofas, that's not dirty and doesn't smell bad.

All these grown-ups around me, and none of them seem to be able to see that that's all I want. Are they that stupid? They keep telling me that I have a lovely new family now, but I don't want it. I just want Mummy.

My new mum keeps telling me that Mummy didn't know how to look after children, and that I wasn't safe. That she and my new daddy need to keep me safe. When they say that, I just drift off and pretend I can't hear them, and then they get cross with me, saying I'm rolling my eyes at them, and it's not a nice thing to do.

Sometimes I call them Alice and George because I don't like saying Mummy and Daddy anymore. It makes them sad, and that makes me feel even more cross and bad inside. They read me lots of books about other little boys and girls who are adopted and are happy with their new families. It always makes me feel sad for their old mummies and daddies. Don't they miss them? One of them made me so mad seeing all their silly smiley faces, so I tore all the pages out.

My mummy knows how to look after me better than my new mummy and daddy. She's the only one who knows that I don't like being tickled apart from one special place on the side of my neck. She's the only one who calls me 'Tigster'. And she'd make me bread with butter and put sugar on it, and we'd eat it in bed as a treat.

Sami said this was because we had no money for heating or food, but I don't care. I liked being in the same bed as Mummy and having cuddles, even if it was a bit smelly. I enjoyed listening to her stories and her telling me about when I was a baby.

My new mummy buys me these fancy 'spensive cakes from the bakery near school with rainbow icing on them. But I think they're stupid and tell her they are, even though I love rainbows. New Mummy got cross when she found one all green and mouldy under my bed. I kept it there because I wanted to give it to Mummy when I saw her again.

When new Mummy and Daddy first came, we went for lots of fun days out. It was really great, and I loved it. They were nice to me. I didn't know that having fun with them meant that I wouldn't be able to see Mummy again, though. And that once I moved in here, they would tell me that I had said goodbye to her forever. I don't 'member that. Now when they buy me nice new toys and clothes, all I can think of is Mummy. I get angry that she wasn't able to have nice things or buy me things that other girls at school had because the mean boyfriend took her money away.

Maybe if I keep being angry and I shout and scream, they'll send me back to Peggy's house. Peggy had too many rules at her house, but at least when I lived there, I got to see Mummy. Sometimes after I've got really cross, new Mummy hugs me, and it feels nice. I cuddle her back, but then I remember Mummy and feel bad like I'm forgetting her, so I hit new Mummy hard, say mean things, and run away just so she won't start thinking I'm her little girl now.

At Peggy's house, Sami came to see me a lot. She told me that my mummy had been sad because she was with a man who wasn't very nice to her and that's why she couldn't look after me properly. I knew about that already because he wasn't nice to me either. But I don't listen to Sami because I think she's silly. I know that Mummy is not with that mean man anymore. She told me at contact. She told me that she wasn't with him so we could live together again soon. I just have to wait.

Adrian

NOW

'These bruises on his face and nose… how did he get them?'

Sami had just sat down next to Joey as he played on the floor. Now, she turned to look at Adrian, her expression changing from calm to concerned.

Picking his way through the toys strewn across the playroom floor, Adrian's heart sank. He sat down heavily on the sofa, putting the two steaming coffees he'd made on the coffee table with a sigh. Joey had been up early and Adrian hadn't slept well, so he'd been looking forward to a cosy morning with his boy. Now, his hopes for an easy meeting with Sami dissipated as quickly as the delicate tendrils of steam that curled into the air.

Sami had arrived promptly at 9 a.m. for her weekly check-in with Joey. These meetings were an essential part of the post-placement support for the adopters and the child, to ensure they were well cared for. The regular check-ins were also meant to address any issues around bonding and attachment in the new family. Adrian usually welcomed the opportunity to chat with Sami about Joey's development. Recently, the meetings had been overwhelmingly positive. Sami had been delighted with the way Adrian and Michael had engaged with the Attachment play therapy support she'd arranged and the way this had clearly shown benefits in how Joey had settled. Today, however, Adrian would rather have been anywhere rather than sitting opposite Sami as she fixed him with her serious gaze.

'I think we need to chat,' he started, anxiety beginning to bubble in his chest. It wasn't that they'd tried to hide the incident from Joey's social worker. He'd been fine and Tegan was okay, they just hadn't wanted to make trouble for themselves, or for Tegan's new family, by going into all the details of what happened at the party. Now, though, he realised that they didn't have a choice. Complete honesty was the only choice he had.

Settling Joey in front of his favourite TV show, Sami and Adrian took their coffees into the dining room. Sami took out her notepad and pen as they sat opposite each other. 'Okay,' she said softly. 'Tell me what happened.'

'Oh, I'm so sorry I wasn't there with you, babe. What did she say? How did it go?'

Adrian managed to get hold of Michael during his lunch hour after Sami left. He had five minutes while Joey was settled eating a fish finger sandwich for lunch. Well, actually, he was busy singing, decimating the bread into tiny pieces, and finger-painting the table with his tomato ketchup, Adrian noticed wearily. I'll deal with that later, he thought as he picked up the phone.

'It's okay. We just got a slap on the wrist for not telling her sooner, which I completely understand. She said she might need to ring and speak to you just to check your version of events which is normal practice, so don't worry. She's also Tegan's social worker, of course, so she's going to call in on them at some point this week, just to check-in, chat to them about how things are going. Between you and me, I think she's already got her concerns about the placement.'

'Yeah, I wouldn't be surprised,' sighed Michael. 'I just hope Alice is okay. She just looked like a shadow of herself at the party. I just wish there was something we could do to help.'

'I know, love, same here. I'll text her in a bit once I've cleaned up the grub monster! I feel like I should just let her know to expect a visit. It's tricky, though, because they've not replied to any of my messages since last weekend. I don't want to seem as though I'm making it worse, I just want them to talk to us. Let us in a bit.'

'All we can do is just let them know we're here for them. I know, it's hard.' A loud ringing reverberated down the phone. 'Anyway, that's the bell, better go. Year 3 history waits for no man! See you later, babe. Love you.'

Becka

NOW

'Do you remember the day we found out we could name them?' Becka reminisced to Charlie, placing her hand on her wife's arm and smiling. That had been a big day in their adoption journey. The day their twins became a part of their family. It had been a poignant moment, Charlie welling up while taking the social workers' telephone call. Becka, not knowing why, holding her hand, concerned.

Now, the two women were sitting closely together at the kitchen table, sipping steaming mugs of coffee, while their boys had their afternoon nap. A rare oasis of calm in otherwise noisy, busy days as parents of rambunctious toddlers.

The quarterly LAC (Looked-After-Child) review meeting held the day before had gone really positively. Everyone involved had expressed their delight at how well the twins had settled in their new home. The IRO (Independent Reviewing Officer) had quietly said to both women as she left the house, 'You're doing a great job with them, well done'. And it felt like the highest of praise. Now they had the green light, it was time for Becka and Charlie to put in the formal application to adopt the children.

They were finding what was really quite a mundane administrative task more emotional than they'd expected. Writing the boys' new names on the form, seeing them in black and white, led them both to look at each other fondly, the enormity of the moment making it one they would remember forever.

The gift of a name. Something so significant when it comes to children and their families. Every birth parent has the right to name their children. Even those whose babies will be collected, swept away by social workers from the hospital, name their babies on the occasion of their birth. It is the one opportunity for the birth parent to impart some lasting gift – an identity, a memory of the child's birth family. A family the child may never get to know.

Adoptive parents give their child many, many things. Love, security, permanence, boundaries. A home, warmth, good food. A future full of opportunities. They choose the child who will join their family, with help from the social workers who hope to create the perfect match.

But one thing adopters can rarely choose is their child's name. These children come with a name and identity already intact. Even the tiniest of new babies have a history that adopters may never fully understand.

Adopters should be fully prepared for this. Indeed, adopters' training courses cover the emotions around this very topic. They work to ensure that new adoptive parents are entirely on board with their children having names they may not have chosen themselves.

'It's obviously something so important, but that was a funny day, wasn't it?' Charlie said, reminding Becka how they'd both had to suppress a giggle during their training when the social worker had asked the group how they'd feel if they were linked with a child called Sonic, for example. The two women had looked at the other couple on the table and smiled when they realised they were all thinking the same thing – that it was quite a cool name!

There are some exceptions to the naming rules. When a child's name is deemed inappropriate, abusive, or distinctive enough to be considered overly identifiable, names are changed. These are safeguarding issues that could threaten an adoption placement's confidentiality and security, and cannot be allowed to be left unaddressed. This was the case with Becka and Charlie's twins.

So angry at the social workers intrusion during her pregnancy, the twins' birth mother had named the babies in spite. Becka was shocked to hear that this happened but was informed by their social workers that, sadly, it wasn't unusual. The babies were named Nosy and Parkers.

The social workers, understandably, deemed it abusive to allow the children to be named as such. Therefore, Becka and Charlie were permitted to call them Parker and Phoenix. It was an unexpected pleasure for them to do this. They both felt that choosing their boys' names enabled them to feel closer to them and allowed them to bond with them right from the start.

The babies were fifteen months old when their new adopters had been told about them, and they had just turned two when they moved home. Early on, a decision was made that Children's Services would allow the boys' new adopters to name them. Known to their foster parents by affectionate pet names up to that point, it was a relief when the matching panel decreed Becka and Charlie to be their new parents. That was the moment their new identities were born.

Alice

NOW

Alice sat with Tegan in the half-light, the bedroom lit solely by a nightlight. Pulling a fleece blanket around Tegan's shoulders, she quietly read one of her favourite childhood books as the atmosphere between mother and daughter slowly calmed. And as the rhythm of Alice's voice rose and fell in the calm of the house, Alice felt stirrings of affection for this cross, confused little girl, who had just arrived in her home. A rush of love, and an urge to protect and nurture this vulnerable child.

The evening had been difficult. Tegan screamed at the top of her voice for nearly an hour when Alice switched off the television at dinner time. Inconsolable at the transition from escapism to the messiness of the real world, the child sobbed while Alice and George held on tight to everything they'd learned. Regulate, regulate, regulate, calm.

It didn't work. Tegan pulled away, screamed and thrashed, repeatedly kicking the living room door in rage while Alice looked on, helpless. Nothing in the books she read had prepared her for the true volatility of Tegan's rages.

How naive she had been, Alice thought, wanting the mother-daughter relationship she always dreamed of. This child had experienced so much trauma. Of course, she had triggers, but so many were what Alice and George considered simple, everyday family life. Helping Tegan feel safe was something they struggled with every day.

Recalling the trauma Tegan had been through was hard for Alice, who had been hoping that once Tegan had settled into their loving family with a solid routine, that she would realise they were enough. But Tegan came from a battleground where she had to fight to survive. Instead of being nurtured, she had been intimidated, purely for being a child. Those scars ran deep and could not be easily healed.

Despite all of this, Tegan had a strong bond with her birth mother, which was the hardest thing for Alice to accept. Piper had pulled herself out of the abusive relationship she was in and got back on her feet. Alice heard from social care that the final contact was cut short because Tegan's mother had told her that she was okay now, she was getting her own place and a job, and that she would fight to get her daughter back.

Tegan was, unsurprisingly, conflicted.

She didn't understand why she couldn't be reunited with her birth mother, and Alice didn't know how to explain it. They were all in an impossible situation.

'Can I write to Mummy one day, to let her know I'm okay?' Tegan once asked, and Alice had no idea what to say. The idea of denying the child this seemed too cruel, but she knew it wasn't allowed.

She'd pulled Tegan towards painting and crafts instead and offered her treats that afternoon, knowing she could do no more than that. Her heart hurt for the situation they were both struggling so hard to understand.

But that night, finally, the little girl settled into bed after exhausting her tears. Alice held Tegan's hand as the girl's body shuddered and relaxed after her last bout of crying. Not yet comfortable with hugs, Tegan kept her distance, her body stiff despite Alice's attempts to comfort her.

Tucking Tegan into bed, Alice pulled the covers lovingly around her neck. The little girl mumbled something, her voice muffled by the weighted teddy squashed against her face.

'Sorry, lovely, I didn't catch that,' Alice whispered, dropping a quick kiss on Tegan's forehead, which was as much affection as she would tolerate.

'You're not my mummy and you never will be.' Louder now, Tegan cried, turning away, covering her face with the duvet,

'Go away. GO AWAY! I hate you. You'll never be my mummy. You won't.'

The girl's body was an angry knot, tension vibrating from every muscle, and the rejection was a fist to Alice's heart. Fragile threads of connection between the two breaking as quickly as they'd been formed.

So difficult to make, so easily broken. Attachments were fragile and the connection was fleeting. The week before, George had snapped, shouting at Tegan after she threw her dinner on the floor for the third night in a row. The girl ran into the living room and hid behind the sofa.

Mortified by this loss of control, George whispered, 'I'm so sorry' as he hugged Alice tight. They stood quietly in the kitchen, holding hands, taking deep breaths, trying to regroup. It was hard to find a way forward with this daughter who felt like a stranger and seemed to sabotage every attempt they made to create an attachment between them.

George sighed. 'This isn't the parent I want to be.' And then, he said, 'This just isn't family life to me, it feels like we're just barely surviving from one day to the next.'

Alice could only nod, her head against the solid chest of her husband. I'm heartbroken for us all that this is just so hard, she thought.

George

NOW

'See you next week, mate. Enjoy your weekend!'

Chance would be a fine thing, George thought grimly. Waving to his colleague, he walked to his car slowly, relishing the few moments of quiet freedom, with the early-spring sun on his face.

These first few moments of warm sunshine that marked this time of year usually lifted his spirits. But now, George had lost track of the number of times lately he'd driven home from work and sat in his car outside his house for five minutes before getting out. Sometimes he even, guiltily, parked around the corner for a while. (Hell, he even felt guilty going to the bathroom at home sometimes these days, knowing how much Alice was facing without him there to take over.)

Once, before going home, he'd switched the radio on. Closing his eyes, he'd got so lost in a song – a throwback from his teens – he'd almost completely forgotten the situation he was currently living in. His heart had sunk when he snapped back to reality. Whatever he did, he always found himself taking several deep breaths before opening the car door. Psyching himself up for the post-work evening shift he knew he was about to face.

Work was busy. It always was. But it didn't bother George. He'd always been laid back. Work was work; home was home. He'd always enjoyed his professional life and home life equally. He had good colleagues, a job he liked (if not loved) and was good at, and a beautiful wife who was his soulmate. Not forgetting their lovely home and ever-faithful dog.

George's life was pretty much complete, but he'd wanted a child to share it with as much as Alice had.

These days, he found himself getting distracted at work, making silly mistakes and snapping at his colleagues. He knew that he was stressing out his team assistant, who he'd noticed whispering in corners with his colleague's PA. No doubt some of the conversations had to do with how short-tempered he'd become lately, and he hated the thought of it. He'd worked really hard to get where he was today. He liked and respected his colleagues and was treated in the same way by them. But he just couldn't seem to maintain his usual affable demeanour lately, and it was getting him down.

So many mornings lately began with him waking up to the sound of Alice sobbing quietly in the en-suite, trying not to let him hear. The week before, he'd returned back from work to see Tegan, tear-stained and red-faced with rage in the front living room window. Before he'd even entered the house, he was alerted to the state of the evening ahead by the sound of her tiny fists banging angrily against the glass. He was then met at the door by an exhausted-looking Alice wanting a hug and two minutes of calm. She told him she'd just informed Tegan it was dinner time, as the child's ear-splitting screams reached them from the other room.

Other times, they didn't manage to be such a united front. He'd only have to look at Alice the wrong way – tired as he was from work – and she took it as blame. As if he was judging her for the state of the house and child when he walked in. He knew his wife had an image in her head of how she'd like the house to be when her husband returned from work, and the current situation did not allow for that dream. For either of them. He'd had his head bitten off a few times lately for suggesting she might want to try a technique he'd read in the books he kept hidden in his desk drawer at work. Trying desperately to find some key that would unlock their daughter's trauma and help them find ways to help and support her. He read in secret, but no longer tried to discuss what he'd read with his increasingly despondent wife. He began to reflect sadly on the difficult journey they'd had to become parents since that day five years ago.

Alice

THEN

Alice remembered that day like it was yesterday.

Five years ago. The day her life changed forever.

Cold, uncomfortable and embarrassed, Alice had undressed with her eyes closed, imagining herself to be anywhere but there. Lying on a beach, tanning and reading the latest bestseller, perhaps. But no, she couldn't entirely ignore the fact that instead, she was lying on a hard hospital bed, thighs open wide, her dignity all but disappearing as a wand-wielding nurse conducted a painful scan of her insides. It was not where she'd ideally be this Friday afternoon.

No, given a choice, Alice would be finishing work early for an infinitely more pleasant reason. Meeting up with her husband to sit outside their favourite cocktail bar in the sunshine as they catch up on their days and watch the world go by would be a much nicer start to the weekend. Highly preferable to this!

Alice recalled, with a pang, how she and her husband had done precisely that the weekend before. It had been a glorious day, and they'd both been able to leave work at 4:00 p.m. Meeting up in the city centre, they'd been happy, contented and looking forward to a relaxing weekend, just the two of them.

Alice had sat down outside the bar where she always did while George went inside to order the drinks. He'd only been gone for a few minutes when a group of new mums, sleeping babies strapped safely to their bodies in a variety of coloured slings, had gathered around her. 'Is this seat taken?' they'd asked as Alice's heart had sunk, settling themselves on the table in front.

George hadn't quite understood why Alice had finished her drink in record time and in silence, dragging him by the hand to leave within minutes. Her positive mood dissipating as she asked to go straight home.

Now, Alice counted down the seconds inside her head until the kindly nurse finished, waiting until she was told she could clean up and put her underwear back on behind the flimsy privacy curtain.

Trying for a baby with George had been such a wonderfully precious secret at first. Alice didn't want to tell anyone that they were trying as it seemed such a magical and private time. Hoping that she'd only tell people – not after too long, surely – once they were pregnant and announcing it to the world, she had no idea at that stage that they'd still be here two years later. Still not pregnant and regularly undergoing intrusive, painful examinations, trying to find out why. Hearing the word that sounded so ugly to Alice's ears – infertility – at every appointment they attended.

Now, the nurse called Alice over, a frown on her serious face. Alice sat down on the plastic chair next to the screen, steeling herself for bad news.

'It's what we expected, I'm afraid, love. There's a lot of scarring inside. That's most likely the reason you're not getting pregnant, I'd say. You said you'd never had any infections before? Are you sure, my dear? I'm so sorry to tell you this, but in all honesty, I think you'd struggle even with IVF to get pregnant with scarring like this.'

And Alice's world as she knew it fell apart in that moment. Her dreams of having a tiny baby of her own crashing around her and her heart breaking just a little bit more than it already had. Dreams of a family with George shattered all around her. Alice knew deep down what had caused this, and she couldn't have regretted it any more than she did, now that she was paying the ultimate price for what had happened.

Becka

NOW

Charlie knew that Becka was a great mum. She was just made for it and had become a mum so naturally; it was now hard to imagine her doing anything else. Her babies completed her body, mind and heart more than she or Charlie could ever have expected. Both women knew that cuddling them, clean, powdered, warm, on the sofa after bath time brought Becka a rush of love and fulfilment that she'd never quite experienced before.

She often told Charlie that it was as if something in her body felt soft and open, full of love, as the boys cuddled against her, heat-seeking in the folds of her body. The way they suckled, thumbs in mouths, heavy little heads leaning sleepily against her.

Her body belonged wholly to these two tiny people right now. Her strong arms to hold them, her softness to comfort them, her heart to regulate them as they attached themselves, seeking connection, to her front. All day, every day. She was theirs to hold. Charlie accepted this and the way their relationship had shifted overnight since the boys arrived.

One twin would always clamber onto Becka's knee while the other slotted under her arm, tightening his tiny, sticky fist around one of her fingers. Becka would often stay like this while the boys napped on top of her. She didn't mind, even though the twins were hardly babies. At two years old, the two of them were often responsible for her numb arms and cramps. She'd post selfies on Instagram with bed-head hair piled loosely in a messy bun on top of her head, with hashtags such as #naptrapped and #mumlife on her #ukadoptioncommunity account. She'd stay there, flicking mindlessly through other mum accounts until her wife lifted sleepy babies from her, her clothes slightly damp and sticky from their heat. Charlie would return to bring her wife steaming cups of tea, patiently demanding snatched moments of her ever-divided attention.

But Charlie could also clearly see that this maternal bliss was tempered with a quiet, bubbling anxiety. Becka was sensitive, an empath. Great for mothering and for art, but a blessing and a curse in so many other ways. One thing she'd never expected when becoming a mother via adoption was the depth of empathy that would grow in Becka for her sons' birth mother. She couldn't help but think of her every time she listened to the boys' giggles, witnessed a first, or pulled them close and sniffed their heads. Every time she noticed one of those moments she wanted to preserve forever, she was painfully aware of the fleeting nature of childhood. Wanting both to be fully in the moment and to take a million photographs. In all those moments, her heart went out to the woman who was these babies' mother, but who saw none of them as they grew.

And with that came the doubt. How could she feel fully authentic, so wholly the mother of these beautiful boys, knowing she'd only ever be their second mum? She knew that she was the one they called Mama, and the one they cried for at night. But nothing could entirely take away this feeling that she was mothering someone else's children, no matter how well she did it.

Charlie lost patience at times, frustrated to see her wife's experience of motherhood so full of worry and doubt. As a former social worker, she was fully aware of the complexities of adoption but also knew the boys were exactly where they needed to be.

'They couldn't even walk, Becka, for fuck's sake. They were filthy, half-starved, lying in a dirty cot and freezing in an unheated house when they were found. Now tell me I should feel sympathy for that woman? I just won't. I fucking won't. Yes, it's hard. It's tough. Looking after twins is hard. But leaving your tiny babies hungry, filthy and cold is not something I can easily forgive. I'm sorry, but that's how I feel.'

Charlie worked hard, loved hard and saw things in black and white. She loved and fiercely protected her little family and had no mixed feelings about the adoption, as far as Becka could tell. Maybe her background as a social worker helped her see adoption as an overwhelmingly positive force for good. Perhaps it was that she didn't want anything to taint the happy family life she and Becka had found with their now sturdy little boys. Maybe it was that simply she believed strongly that the proof of a mother is in what you do, and not merely based on what can be read in your blood.

She had sighed, looking at Becka's face, her wife's eyes full of tears as she wept for the birth family the boys had left behind.

'You know I love you. I love your big heart. I love how much you care. I do! I just want you to enjoy this. To let go a bit. You're their mummy, love. Not her. You're the only one they want. They don't even know who she is, they wouldn't recognise a picture of her, and they wouldn't even look twice if they saw her in the street, you know?!'

But she knew as she said it that somehow, to Becka, that was almost worse.

THEN

'If you're at home like me on New Year's Eve (although judging by the photos on your profile, I very much doubt it!), I thought you might appreciate a distraction from endless scrolling through messages that start with 'hey babes' and end with a kiss, without anything else in between.

So, here's a bit about me. My name's Charlie, and I recently left my job as a social worker to go independent, which means my stress levels have dramatically improved! I have a lot more time to indulge my hobbies, including walking, playing squash, eating cheese, and drinking good red wines...'

Pounding dance music in the overcrowded bar vibrated against the toilet stall walls where Becka was sitting, hunched over on the loo, trying to make the room stop spinning. As her stomach heaved, she thought, 'I'm too old for this,' wondering if her party-loving friends would notice if she just went home. Her head was swimming, and she was seriously regretting the last shot of lurid pink vodka she'd drunk as the clock struck midnight.

Scrolling through her phone, squinting slightly, and putting off the moment she'd have to return to the heaving, sticky-floored bar, Becka was pleasantly surprised to see a notification flashing blue on the dating app she'd downloaded just a few weeks before.

Opening it and reading the message from Charlie, she smiled. She didn't know Charlie yet, but she had a feeling from her message that she very soon would. And she was right, it did make a delightful change to receive a message that was thoughtful, well written and engaging, despite Becka having to squint to read it through vodka-bleary eyes.

There was something cosy and homely about Charlie's message that made her want to go straight home, put on pyjamas and drink a hot cup of tea in bed while she replied, instead of being here in this sweaty, sticky bar that had begun to smell very slightly of vomit.

Yuck, thought Becka, time to get home. Ignoring the way her head spun, she stumbled up the bar's stairs onto the street to flag down a taxi, impatient to shuffle onto its warm, leather seats and look at Charlie's profile, and read her words one more time as the cab sped her home through the darkened streets.

One week later, she'd been excitedly preparing for their first date. Unlike her previous dates, which had always been held in bars and involved copious amounts of alcohol, she and Charlie met nervously in a cute little coffee shop tucked away behind the high street. Over tea and cake, they'd chatted for hours, feeling comfortable with one another straightaway.

And the first time I stayed over at her house, I knew I was home, Becka thought. I'd never felt so calm and safe anywhere before in my life, and I knew from that moment that we'd be wives. And look at us now, married with children, and I couldn't be happier.

NOW

Reminiscing on how far they'd come, Becka tucked her little boys up in their beds for their afternoon nap, after holding them tight for a little longer than usual. I need these cuddles more than them today, she thought, after a challenging morning. Both boys were cutting their two-year-old molars and were grumpy, red-cheeked and unsettled, making for a long morning.

Warm milk, Calpol and lots of cuddles had calmed them enough to nap, and once their breathing settled into the even rhythm of sleep – a minor miracle, with both twins napping at the same time – Becka padded downstairs quietly. Time for some self-care, she thought, ignoring the one million other jobs she could be doing.

She loved her two little whirlwinds, but naptime was always welcome, particularly on days like today when there was so much going on in her head. Brewing a strong, sweet coffee, she grabbed some chocolate from the cupboard and settled into the cosy sofa in the corner of the kitchen. It was early afternoon and a low sun filled the room, bathing her in its warmth.

She picked up her phone and opened a blog post she'd saved to read later – an adoptive mum's perspective on unconditional love and her five-year-old son. Adrian had sent the link to the WhatsApp group earlier that day, commenting: *'Saw this and thought of you all! xx'*.

Now, savouring the calm with the comforting hit of chocolate and her sweet coffee, Becka began to read, always fascinated to find out more about the experiences of other adopters.

Unsurprisingly, on a day filled with so much emotion, the first line of the blog brought a tear to her tired eyes:

'I went into my son's bedroom this morning to wake him up, and to soak up some sleepy cuddles. It's my favourite time of the day. My son sat on my knee, put his warm arms around my neck and said to me: "Mummy, I didn't love you for a while. But I do now."

My boy is loving, sweet, affectionate and kind. When he hurts himself, nothing quite makes it better than a cuddle with Mummy. I do not doubt his love or need for me. I am his mum. If he were my birth child, I may have struggled with what he said, but as an adoptive mum, it makes my heart sing.

Early on, he learned to be good. To be cute, sweet and adored by everyone, to keep people happy. He had many a cute mannerism employed to keep himself safe.

During introductions, my son would run up to me every time he saw me, arms up in the air, shouting "Mummy!" until I picked him up, covered him in kisses, and spun him around.

It was lovely and brought tears to my new-mama eyes, but I also knew that it was a survival mechanism. It kept him safe, loved and wanted.

We don't see these behaviours anymore. We see all of him, him at his best and at his worst. And we love him all the same.

I can only imagine how scary it must be for him now to speak his truth so fully. I never want him to grow up feeling he can't say how he feels for fear of upsetting people and then suffering the consequences of that. I know how people-pleasing feels and how life-limiting it can be.

So, I couldn't be prouder to know that now he feels safe, secure and confident enough in our love to say this to us. To be truthful and honest. To be sure of our unconditional love and be brave enough to challenge it.

This unexpected interaction with my son this morning showed me the meaning of unconditional love. "I didn't love you for a while, but now I do." I'm so proud that we got here, gorgeous boy.'

Sami

NOW

Sami turned to smile and wave goodbye to Piper, who was standing proudly and smiling on the doorstep of her new home, her hand lovingly caressing her now-huge bump. Sami had spent the morning finally helping her move into the new furnished housing association flat that they'd visited together five months before.

Sami had spent a frustrating few months trying to move the paperwork along more quickly, aware of the clock ticking as the birth of Piper's baby became ever more imminent. As the two women had stepped over the threshold, she'd seen a tear fall from Piper's eye before it was hastily rubbed away. It had been an emotional moment for both of them.

Now Sami got back into her car, her back aching from the lifting and carrying. She was tired, but happy that the move had gone so smoothly. Piper loved the new place. Throughout the morning, the informal chats reassured Sami that Piper was doing everything she could to make a safer and happier life for herself and her new baby. She was just relieved that they'd been able to arrange all of the paperwork in time for Piper to move in before her new baby arrived, which could be at any time now.

But despite the positive morning, Sami was preoccupied, already thinking of the next job on her to-do list. While Piper had looked happily around the new flat, placing her meagre possessions in the drawers and on surfaces, Sami noticed an email notification pop up on her mobile phone. Opening it now, she saw that the Adoption Support Worker in her team had emailed, informing her that Alice and George had cancelled Tegan's first two Attachment play therapy sessions, but she hadn't given a reason why.

These evidence-based play sessions formed part of the adopter support package set up for the family at the start of the placement. They were considered mandatory by the placing authority for which Sami worked. The social worker frowned deeply. This wasn't like Alice, who was probably one of the most diligent, organised, and eager-to-please of all the adopters they had on their books. Thinking back, she also realised that Alice had failed to pick up the phone the last time she'd called to check in on the family. This led Sami to add a note to the family's file marked: *'has not engaged with support services to help the parents and child post-placement'*. Irritated, Sami searched for Alice's number now and tried to get through to her, her knee jigging distractedly as she listened to the dial tone. Everything she had to get done that day ran like a constant mantra of stress through her head.

Alice

NOW

From under the duvet, Alice could hear the muffled but insistent ringing of the mobile phone tucked in bed beside her but couldn't bring herself to answer it. She knew it was probably important, but she was so numb at the moment, it didn't seem to matter. Messages and calls had gone unanswered for days now, despite Alice spending much of her time glued mindlessly to her phone. She scrolled in desperate hope of finding something that would help drag her out of this hole she'd fallen so deeply into. She lethargically, yet compulsively, refreshed adopter groups on Facebook and Instagram with no energy to post or reply. The prep group WhatsApp had been muted the week before, and its silence left Alice calmer, lonelier and bereft in equal measure. She had no words to describe what she was going through, and no energy left to connect.

That morning, it had taken nearly two hours to get Tegan up, out of bed, dressed and ready to school. After handing the angry child to her teacher, Alice had rushed away from the other parents for fear that she'd break down, messily, noisily, in front of them.

The effort of getting the girl to school had taken every ounce of energy she had. She longed for the quiet security of her car to let the tears fall. Her arms hurt from where her girl had battled, fought and hit her. Her whole body was pounding with stress and adrenaline. Her breath was short from anxiety. Her head still spun with echoes of screams and shouts that had woken her, dragging her from bed before 6:00 a.m.

Rubbing her sweaty palms on her grubby tracksuit bottoms, she caught a glimpse of herself. Greasy hair, eyes sunken into dark shadows, ringed with red. She didn't recognise her own reflection.

Through heavy, sobbing sighs, trying to catch her breath, she'd driven slowly home. Ignoring the state of her usually tidy, welcoming home, she'd taken a family-sized bar of chocolate and a large coffee to bed and stayed there all day. She struggled to remember when she'd last washed or dressed in something other than leggings. She pulled on one of George's unwashed t-shirts because it smelled like him. Then huddled under the duvet, wishing she could hibernate and re-emerge when life got a little bit easier, pushing away unwelcome memories as they crowded her thoughts in the silence.

THEN

Home, I need to get home.

What was it she'd just left?

Please, just let me get safely home.

The back door closed quietly with a soft click behind her as Alice crept out of the unfamiliar house into the early morning light, something urgent pushing at her from inside, telling her to run.

Once outside, she heard birds singing happily around her, but her head throbbed painfully with this slightest of sound, and the soft glow of the dawning sun made her suddenly want to cry.

Desperate to get home and crawl into a burning hot shower, Alice took rushed steps as she headed for home. She longed to curl up in the peace, quiet and safety of her bedroom to help her make some sense of what had happened, but the short walk home felt so far, so hard, and so painful to make.

Her head thrummed with panic as she almost broke into a run, something desperate inside her telling her to get away. Cold air clawed at her skin as she shivered in the flimsy party clothes she'd worn the night before, that now felt dirty, tainted and unwelcome on her quivering, shaking body.

What had happened in there?

Why did she feel, all of a sudden, as though the very heart of her had been ripped out?

Why did she feel so crushed, so cold, and so broken inside?

Why did everything hurt?

Her head throbbed, and she choked back the sobs threatening to spill as she thought of how she'd bravely moved out of Axel's home the month before. After the way he'd isolated and beaten her down, it had been the most challenging step Alice had ever had to take, but now she kicked herself, angry, frustrated tears dashing to her red, tired eyes, for messing up everything she'd worked so hard to rebuild. He'd called the night before, begging her for another chance, and like an idiot, she'd let him back into her head.

'It's a party,' he said. 'Loads of people will be there. What could happen at a party?'

She'd be safe, and he was sorry.

'Let me show you how sorry I am, firefly. I can't sleep without you; I just want to see you again. We'll go to the party, have some fun, and if you don't have a good time, we'll leave it there. Go our separate ways. What do you say?'

Loneliness and lack of self-esteem had left her vulnerable and desperate for company. She'd said yes. All of her friends had gradually drifted away in the Axel years, and he knew it. He knew she wouldn't have any other plans that Friday night.

It was supposed to be fun. So why, now, did she feel a swelling thrum of panic spreading through her body when she tried to recall the events of last night? Why did her body ache and hurt with every movement? Why couldn't she remember? What was the creeping sense of horror now gathering in the front of her mind, making her want to scream and scream in this empty, early-morning street?

They were the same streets that had led her to the party, anxious but cautiously optimistic the night before, after Axel had turned up at her house. He had been his old charming self. Brandishing her favourite wine, dressed smartly and smelling sensuously of her favourite aftershave, he had pulled her close for a kiss. And Alice, despite herself, was caught by the familiar pull of attraction. She smiled, touched up her lipstick, and laughingly claimed that she didn't need a coat, letting herself be taken by the hand into the balmy, summer evening.

Pushing the door to the party open, a heavy drum beat filling their ears, Axel grinned at her, pulling her in tightly to his side.

'Relax, firefly. We'll have some fun tonight, you'll see.'

Stumbling into the front room, Alice was surrounded by a shadowy blur of people, drinks and laughter. Music filled her ears, and a drink was pushed into her hand.

But now Alice thought back, she had realised quickly she was the only girl. And the men were faces, hands, and mouths that leered a little too close for comfort. The room was dark, and the drinks were a little too strong.

Anxiety building and wanting to leave, she searched for Axel, but like a house of mirrors, no matter how hard she looked, he couldn't be found. And, not knowing the place or the people, she let herself sink into the sofa, gulping back alcohol to lessen her fears until she was slumped next to a bad-smelling man whose name she didn't know, but who put his arm around her all the same.

And then she was offered something that she thought was MDMA powder. It appeared in front of her while she was fuzzy from the vodka that had softened her senses. All Alice could think of at that moment was that she needed something to get her through this night, and she'd taken it before, and it had been fun. Maybe it would be again.

In the early days when she was young and naïve, Axel had introduced her to the magic pills and powders that were part of bringing an evening to life. The party pills that made her spin and dance – her body soft, fluid and light as a feather – as the music picked her up and spun her around. Everything felt intense. The kisses on her lips, a night that seemed to last forever, and the fierce joy of being young and in love.

Back then, everyone they'd met had been a friend, and everything they'd done had been fun. At parties, when she'd danced, happy and carefree, he'd stood and stared at her, only her.

'My beautiful firefly,' he'd said, spinning her around.

Now, stumbling, alone, into her cold, empty kitchen after fumbling the key in the lock with shaking hands, Alice's stomach began to lurch in the stark early morning light as she remembered the last words she'd heard in Axel's voice. His familiar, imposing figure had appeared right behind her moments after powerful particles of unknown white powder had been propelled willingly up through her nose, on course to her brain.

And the last words she remembered him saying were delivered as he laughed, cruelly with his friends, these men she didn't know, and she knew with a sudden lurch of fear that they were laughing at her.

'She thinks it's MDMA. It's ketamine, stupid bitch.'

Becka

NOW

'How must she be feeling today? I can't imagine what it must be like for her,' mused Becka thoughtfully to her wife, cuddled cosily next to her in bed.

It was Mother's Day, and the still-sleepy women were in bed, a toddler on each knee, crumbs covering the sheets, and the boys sticky from the chocolate pastries they'd all consumed, messily, just moments before. But Becka didn't care about the mess, these were the precious moments of parenting she'd always dreamed of. I'm finally a mum, and I love it, she thought, gratitude filling her heart. Crumbs and all.

Playfully pushing away Parker's chocolatey kisses as he leant in for a hug, Charlie turned to her wife, squeezing Becka's hand tight. Knowing her wife as well as she did, she didn't have to ask who 'she' was. It could only be their sons' birth mother.

'I just hope she's getting the support she needs,' Charlie replied, kindly. 'It certainly is a bittersweet day for us. Our happiness is her sadness, and I know I don't say it often enough, but I don't take that lightly. Stepping into her shoes to parent these two is an enormous responsibility, and some days, I do wish she were around to see just how amazing they both are.'

As Charlie spoke, Becka was reminded of a quote she'd read about adoptive parenting. It said, *'They are mine in a way they will never be hers. They are hers in a way they'll never be mine,'* and never did this quote seem more apt than it did at this moment.

The wives didn't know much about the twins' birth mother, Keira, only that she was young, had been in and out of trouble with the police as a teenager, and had her first child at fifteen. The twins followed when Keira was eighteen.

All three children had gone on to be adopted, having been removed from Keira's care at the time of the twins' birth. Alarm bells had rung when Keira left the three-year-old unattended in her local toy shop while taking a taxi to the hospital in labour. Social services had been alerted when the pale, dirty child was still nestled in the play area with a teddy she'd taken from the shelf, fast asleep and sucking her thumb at closing time.

Becka certainly didn't condone what she'd done. Still, her heart went out to the young woman, barely out of childhood herself, who had no other option but to leave her child in what she considered to be a safe place when she was about to give birth.

What must have been running through her mind to make her do that? How desperate must she have been?

Now, Becka knew that Parker and Phoenix were her sons. There was no doubting their love or need for her and Charlie, but their blue eyes, the curls in their hair, and the matching birthmarks on their knees came from their birth mother. They might not have kept Keira's surname, or have her arms around them when they cry, but they were made perfectly by her, and Becka and Charlie will never forget what a gift it is, to parent another woman's child. Becka knew she would never be able to compete with the role she'd had in their lives.

Without their birth mum, Parker and Phoenix would never be here, in Becka's arms. And she thanked this woman, a stranger to them all, with everything she had every day for the privilege of being able to raise these gorgeous boys.

The day before, Becka had been feeling low and a little bit sorry for herself, texting Charlie to complain about their plans being cancelled. Charlie's parents had taken a last-minute trip abroad, not thinking of Mother's Day at all, and

Becka's mum had fallen ill a few days before, postponing their get-together to a later date.

Since the boys were placed with them, Becka and Charlie had both dreamed of dressing them up in cute outfits and descending on their parents' homes on Mother's Day bearing cake, prosecco and gifts. It would have been their first celebration of new motherhood, a precious memory they'd never forget. Now it was a missed opportunity that Becka felt, grumpily, they'd never get back.

Now she felt embarrassed for having such frivolous concerns when she reflected on the devastation that a mother with empty arms must feel. A mother who gave birth to such beautiful boys and who would never have the chance to see them again. It broke Becka's heart to think of how painful this must be, to have empty arms where your babies should be on Mother's Day.

But despite their Mother's Day not being quite what they'd dreamed of, it was, at the same time, more than Becka could have ever asked for. Smiling, she pulled her two boys close as they giggled and jostled for space between her and her wife. She loved her life with her little family, sticky hands in the bed and all.

'I hope that one day, they'll all be able to meet up, you know? I want our boys to see her, to say they've had a wonderful life, and for her to see them and be proud. To see how well they've turned out and for her to have had a good life too. I want that more than anything for our sons.'

But for now, these boys are all ours, Becka thinks. She holds her wife's hand tightly, kissing her cherished babies on the tops of their soft downy heads, and thinks, how did I get so lucky to be loved by you all?

Alice

THEN

Optimistically, and despite the nurse's warnings, Alice and George had proceeded with several rounds of IVF treatment in the hope of becoming pregnant. Determined not to let the mistakes of the past with Axel ruin her chances to become a mother, Alice had embarked upon fertility treatment with determined enthusiasm.

As a young, married, heterosexual couple, she and George were eligible for two rounds of IVF funded by their GP's local authority, but Alice's hopes plummeted when the first two tries ended firstly in failure, then in the fleeting joy of fragile pregnancy.

The latter resulted in a devastating early loss of twin embryos followed by an uncomfortable and distressing hospital procedure when the miscarriage did not complete naturally.

When she'd left the hospital, George was there to pick her up. Seeing the pain written all over her face, he gently took Alice's hand and said, 'Enough, now.' And Alice, feeling slightly broken inside, had not been able to do anything but nod, sadly, knowing he was right. It wasn't to be their last try though. Once she had recovered, they would try again, just once more. Just to be sure.

But now, sitting in her living room for yet another probing adoption assessment meeting with Cara, the first nurse's words rang sadly in Alice's ears.

'I very much doubt you'll be able to become pregnant with scarring like this, love, even with the help of IVF. Are you sure you've never had an infection?'

The first few weeks after that last party with Axel, ten years before, had passed in a blur for Alice. Flooded with embarrassment, shame and disgust at herself for letting

Axel back into her life, she told no one about what had happened that night. Feeling sick to her stomach at not knowing entirely what had happened herself, she called in sick to work and spent a day huddled under her duvet, then deep in a hot bath, trying to wash away the shame that felt like a layer of grime on her skin. But nothing could entirely wash away all the complicated emotions that threatened to overwhelm her. So, after that day, she got up, went to work and tried to carry on as if nothing had happened, not knowing what to do or who to trust with this horrible knowledge building within her.

That was ten years ago. A box of emotions that had been silenced, packed away and pushed to the back of her mind, never again to be opened. Until now.

Alice and George's Stage 2 assessments had already taken a long time to complete. Alice had become discouraged when Cara had informed them that she'd be adding in an extra three sessions to discuss Alice's emotions around IVF, pregnancy loss, and infertility following the disclosures Alice had made in their first individual meeting.

Alice knew it was essential for them to work through it all, but sometimes, the overwhelming impatience to become a mum after everything they'd already been through felt too much for her and she could scream with frustration at all of these meetings that seemed never-ending.

But she was determined to become a mum, even if it meant opening up and discussing the most painful parts of her life so far. So, she fixed a smile on her face and went to greet Cara.

'Hi Alice, how are you today? Ready to get started?'

George

NOW

'But Tegan isn't a baby, though, Auntie.'

'Och, don't start me wi'that, hen. Baby blues is baby blues – don't matter t'age of t'bairn now. Is Alice awake a night? Is the gel screaming an' crying all the long livin' day? Is t'house a mess? Can she not get five minutes to hersen? Mark my words it's baby blues, no doubt about it.'

'Okay, it certainly sounds like it. But what can I do to help? She's just not herself at all. One day she won't get out of bed, barely saying a word, and the next she's cleaning and baking like the Queen herself is coming to tea. And she's so exhausted all the time. I'm so worried, Jean.'

'Talkin'. That's the only thing that helped in my day, love. Talkin' to mams. Don't let her sit there stewin' in muck of 'house all day long. Get art there, get talking, laughin', cryin', drinkin' whatever – just tellin' others bout it. Only way through it. All mams gerrit – wake up one mornin', proper vexed, thinkin' their child's ruined their life. I were jiggered, I were mi'sen wi' my four – woulda give 'em back if I could! Told my John that, many a time too, mark my words. I were proper narky wi'im. It's normal. Next thing, you're fightin' off anyone dares come near that bairn. She's a good'un – she'll be reet, you'll see, hen.'

The reassuring warmth of Jean's words was like getting a tight bear hug through the phone. That particular day, George felt desperate and low after finding Alice obsessively cleaning an already pin-neat kitchen in the dark, long before Tegan was due to get up. The tins were lined up in alphabetical order in the cupboards, and she leapt up to clear his coffee cup and wipe the non-existent stain underneath when he'd barely finished drinking. Fake cheer was plastered over her face as she hugged George quickly,

139

a brittle grin on her lips. And she said a quick goodbye, as if she were scared of melting into tears if he held her too long. It was the Friday before Mother's Day and George didn't know what to do about that. Whether to celebrate or not. He knew the expectation of the day was weighing heavy on his wife's mind and didn't know what to do to help. He thought of Tegan at school and how she was probably expected to make a card for Alice, all the while missing her birth mum. George couldn't even begin to imagine how she must be feeling, but his heart hurt with the enormity of what they were all going through. He just wished he knew what was for the best.

George had climbed into his car, while scrolling through numbers in his phone, wanting to call someone for help, but not knowing where to turn. He loved his mum so much, but he was scared of what she'd say, now that things were so difficult.

In the end, he'd turned to Jean, a family friend he'd met when he'd been at University in Yorkshire. Kindly and welcoming, Jean must have only been in her late forties, but she seemed much older and wiser than that.

She'd lived next door to a house full of students, but she'd never once complained about the parties, the noise, or the late nights they'd kept. She was a kind of surrogate auntie to George and his friends, so much so that all four boys ended up calling her 'Auntie' at the end of three years at uni. She was one of the reasons they kept the same student house throughout their degrees, not wanting to move away from such a great source of support. This meant that the four boys ended up with the closest friendships and lifelong support in Jean. She was always there for a quick chat over the fence when they were lonely and missing home, the kettle was always on for a strong cup of tea if they needed support, and she was full of ready pearls of wisdom if they lacked parental guidance. George knew that Jean's down-to-earth, straight-talking brand of wisdom was just what he needed right then.

Cheered by her words, he pulled his mobile phone from his pocket and went to message the prep group WhatsApp for the first time since Tegan had arrived home: *'Hey guys, how's things? Hope you're all doing well. We've definitely been having some tough days lately, but we're taking it one day at a time. Would love to hear how you're all doing! Hope parenting is treating you well.'*

He couldn't seem to bring himself to share the truth. Not just yet.

Adrian

NOW

'It'll be fine, don't worry!' Adrian smiled, pushing Michael out the door to work as Joey screamed behind him.

It was a Saturday, but Michael had to go into school for an open day, a change to routine that had already impacted their son's fragile emotions. Knowing this, Adrian squatted down to his son's level and gently held Joey's pummelling fists, keeping them firmly away from his face as he spoke calmly, remembering how his training had taught him about the skill of 'wondering' in moments like these.

'I wonder if Daddy going to work early has made Joey feel a bit wobbly today,' he said, watching for signs of acknowledgement in Joey's angry, little face. 'When you feel wobbly inside, sometimes it makes you feel like shouting at Dadda. Now, let's think. What can we do instead of shout?'

To Adrian's surprise, the boy took a deep, shuddering breath and calmed enough for Adrian to pick him up, throw him over his shoulder and run with Joey jiggling on his back as if riding a horse around the living room. Soon they collapsed, giggling, on the floor, Adrian's arms grasped tightly around his son. The moment was saved.

Moments like this were becoming more frequent. Times when Adrian, calling on therapeutic parenting, connected with his son's emotional needs and defused his behaviour that way, instead of listening helplessly as the boy screamed and hit out to express his distress.

Parenting him certainly wasn't easy, Adrian reflected. There had been many times when it had taken both him and Michael to undress Joey for bed as he fought them, aiming his fists at their faces and his little feet at their chests. It was hard to search for playful responses when exhausted, or to find reserves of patience when they really wanted five minutes of peace. But finally, they saw the results and started bonding with their son, and Adrian felt like they were becoming a happy little family.

The week before, Michael had trapped his own fingers in the car door after strapping Joey into his car seat. The little boy's face crumpled with concern for his dad, asking if he was okay, and offering to sing him a song to make him feel better before launching into an earnest rendition of 'Ants, ants, ants on your arm'. The empathy Joey had shown had brought tears to Michael's eyes, and Adrian knew it had been a vital bonding moment for the two of them. Both men knew that empathy was often a complex emotion for adopted children to express, so they were incredibly proud of Joey for showing this to his new dads in what were still relatively early days. With all his kindness, cheekiness and spirit, Joey's personality was emerging, and it filled Adrian's heart with joy.

Parenting was a learning curve for both men. As a teacher, Michael was used to setting rules, imposing boundaries and consequences, and following them through. He was experienced in his profession and able to run a well-organised classroom. Throughout the adoption assessment process, he often referred to his experience as a teacher to reflect on how he may parent a child, and it was true that he had much childcare experience to draw on.

However, using therapeutic parenting was very different from teaching in a classroom, and Michael had struggled to adapt his style at first. Now, though, inspired by Adrian's success, Michael was developing a different parenting style with daily practice. Naming the need, parenting playfully, and using compassion to explore the feelings behind the behaviour had become second nature to the two dads, and their relationship with Joey was improving all the time as a result.

Far from my childhood, thought Adrian. Never knowing whether his mum would be up or down on any given day had led Adrian to fear extreme emotions, and avoid talking about his feelings, preferring to say 'I'm fine' whenever pushed on them. While exploring this in-depth in his adoption assessments, Adrian had become more aware that his emotional range was limited due to his childhood, something that he was exploring every day now as he learned to unpack the often complicated and changeable feelings of his three-year-old son.

Alice

THEN

'Welcome to Cyprus!' smiles the cheerful customs officer as Alice and George step excitedly off the plane into a 40-degree heat that feels like entering a sauna, sweat prickling at their brows.

'We're here! I can't believe we're here!' says Alice, squeezing George's hand, squinting in the sunlight. 'Let's make a baby!'

Just a couple of months before, Alice had been submerged in a rapidly cooling bath at home, scrolling aimlessly through her phone.

She was forming a plan. George was sitting on the end of the tub while she poured in more hot water and sank below the bubbles. 'What would you say if we went abroad?' Alice asked, reappearing suddenly from below the water, an idea forming excitedly in her mind that she couldn't wait to share.

George looked at her, more cautious, and raised an eyebrow, waiting. Alice knows him and is sure he'll be on board, but she wants to infect him with the bubbling enthusiasm rushing from her words. She grins. It's a crazy half-formed plan, but with a bit of persuasion, she's sure he'll take this massive leap of faith with her. He has to.

After their first miscarriage, Alice and George lost hope. Pragmatic and financially cautious, they realised that further IVF was likely to fail. Despondent, Alice looked to the Instagram TTC community for support, creating a profile and sharing her feelings with friends. After a while, she connected with a couple who had travelled to Cyprus for IVF, and were now pregnant with their first baby. And even better, the clinic offered a startlingly high success rate.

Inspired by this couple's story, George and Alice felt their excitement building as disbelief turned into 'okay, so we're doing this!', and they began to form a plan that could change their lives forever. Alice and George eagerly contacted the clinic to be told they could book flights and have treatment within the next couple of months. After the journey they'd been on, this seemed too easy, almost unbelievable. But, looking at each other laughing, Alice persuaded George to go for it. What have they got to lose?

Navigating various websites, they ordered the medicine, booked their flights and accommodation in a rush of excitement, and tacked the Cyprus trip to the end of a European holiday they'd already booked. As they paid for it all, they held hands, knowing this was the most impulsive and scary thing they will probably ever do together. A real adventure – the beginning of a family.

'One way or another, this summer together is going to be memorable,' smiled Alice. 'Our European adventure!'

A month or so later, Alice and George were relaxing on a white rocky beach on the south coast of France. Life was good, the sky is cloudless and blue, the sea is beautiful, and they've both taken a dip in its sun-warmed waves.

They had spent the last two weeks waking early to meander lazily to the bakery around the corner to pick up buttery, flaky croissants for breakfast, and then eating them slathered in jam on the front step of their tiny holiday home. Days have been spent running in and out of the waves, sunbathing, eating ice creams, baguettes and cheese. Alice is sun-kissed and relaxed. The perfect conditions to make a baby, Alice muses, imagining the vitamin D seeping into her skin as she stretches out on her towel.

In less than forty-eight hours, they're due to return to England, stay a night, then board another flight to Cyprus the following day. Nerves are setting in, and Alice feels an excited, panicky buzz building in her belly. She can't wait to get to Cyprus, but at the same time, she obsesses about having missed a potentially vital part of the planning.

Having been on holiday while they've made the arrangements – enjoying their sun-kissed idyll in a tiny cottage in France, accompanied by good food and the occasional glass of good red wine – renders the whole experience more surreal, more dream-like, than it would have been planning at home.

Soon, they will be in British Cyprus and cross over to the Turkish side to get to the fertility clinic. Do they need a visa? They haven't got one. Have they got long enough left on their passports? Will they let them cross the border? Is the clinic legit? Have they sent money to a scam?

Worries multiply and sitting under the sun in this scenic corner of France, Alice feels cut off from the real world, as though she's entering uncharted waters without a map. Turning up in a country neither of them has ever visited, with a language they don't speak, to attend a fertility clinic neither of them has any knowledge of feels crazy to them both.

The next day, Alice and George return to Birmingham and check into an airport hotel for the night, but neither sleeps. George texts previously kept-private plans to their families. In the morning, bleary-eyed, they eat a cooked breakfast and climb aboard their second flight in two days in a blur of sleep deprivation and nerves.

Arriving in Cyprus, the sun is fierce on the chalky white buildings and Alice and George look around in wonder at their new surroundings as they wait in the taxi line, fatigue fighting with anticipation. It's hard to remember that they're still on holiday when they're focused on such an important mission – they're here to make a baby.

Nerves intensify when they give the address of the accommodation to the Cypriot taxi driver who doesn't recognise the street name and, after a winding journey through twisty streets, drops them off on a street corner in the blazing hot sunshine. Alice and George pull their suitcases into a pile on the ground, bewildered, with no idea where to go.

Seeing their confusion, a kindly passer-by looks at the address, which had been hastily scribbled on paper for the taxi driver, and attempts to help them. Between them, they come across the management office for their apartment.

Exhausted from the journey, Alice and George are delighted by the manager's cheerful charisma as he enthuses in broken English about the accommodation's facilities, showing them around.

That night, they venture to the beachfront for a pizza, listening to the waves rushing in a gentle, persistent rhythm on the sand, immersed in a blanket of summer heat. They talk excitedly about what faces them the following day and walk back hand-in-hand after dinner, knowing it will be difficult to sleep that night. Later, they administer the meds provided by the clinic (nothing says 'let's make a baby' more than having your husband stab you in the butt with an intramuscular injection, Alice muses, thinking of a funny story for Instagram) and watch a Netflix series on their laptop, happy to have a taste of home in this entirely strange experience they've found themselves in.

The taxi arrives early the next day, winding them out of the busy city and into the sparse, open countryside. Instead of the lush green hills and trees of home, the landscape is pale, sun-bleached and bare, making it feel unfamiliar. Alice's nerves bubble in her throat as they reach the British/Turkish Cypriot border. She hands over her passport, not knowing why she's so worried, but it's soon returned to her and they are waved across.

Everything is efficient and easy at the clinic, and Alice is walked through the process with ease. They do this every day; they know the drill. Alice pauses to look up at the imposing hospital building with the 'Miraculous IVF' sign attached discretely to the door. This could be where our miracle begins, she thinks.

Once upstairs, she is shown a picture of the embryos destined for her waiting womb – two beautiful, perfect donor embryos from unknown Cypriots in their twentysomethings, chosen to maximise their chances of success. Young, fresh, healthy embryos. With overwhelming gratitude, Alice thinks of the young people these genes came from and tries to imagine their eyes and hair. Their smiles. Their lives. Could one of these combinations of their perfect, young genes be our child?

It is all over quickly, and ten days after returning from Cyprus, Alice begins to wake in the night, needing to pee more often, feeling nauseated. She feels different, but isn't able to explain how.

She hides in the bathroom, finding it impossible to believe that after all this time, it could have worked. She pees on a test, pushes it away from her, hides it under a towel, runs to the kitchen to make a coffee. She tries her best to guard her heart before she creeps back to the bathroom. Her heart is pounding in her throat, sweat is coating her palms, and there is a heavy sickness in her stomach. It can't be.

She looks.

It is.

One word written as clear as day on the digital screen.

Tears prick her eyes as she blinks, unbelieving.

Pregnant.

A miracle.

They're going to have a baby.

****

'Okay, ladies, take your places, let's get started!'

A gently upbeat remix of a popular song filled the dance studio as the yoga class participants laid their brightly coloured mats in a horizontal pattern facing the teacher, ready to start their weekly class. The instructor, sitting in lotus pose facing the room, smiled over at Alice and warmly welcomed her to the studio.

It was Alice's first time at yoga, and she was feeling a little nervous. She needn't have worried, though. The receptionist of the leisure centre greeted her as if she were a regular, and other participants engaged her in conversation as they waited in line to enter the studio. Still, being unused to physical exercise recently, Alice doubted her ability to keep up with the class.

Years of infertility, IVF, early pregnancy and miscarriage had left Alice feeling uncomfortable and under-confident in her body. The latest miscarriage – the precious Cyprus twins – had half broken Alice, and her body held the scars.

Just a couple of months before, Alice and George had returned home elated after discovering that their holiday pregnancy, their perfect, top-grade donor embryos had resulted in twins and, excitedly booking an eight-week scan, they'd waited impatiently for the day to come around.

Lying in the scan room, her husband holding her hand, the scan technician was barely able to hold back her emotions, and Alice's excitement quickly turned to grief as she and George heard the words no pregnant couple ever wants to hear.

'I can't find a heartbeat.'

And just like that, time stood still.

Alice wanted to close her ears and eyes, and shut off all her senses, so she could somehow avoid experiencing any more of this moment that she'd feared so much. She then suddenly began feeling foolish and awkward, lying on the bed with the scan still on the screen, the mocking sadness of the womb that couldn't sustain these tiny, tiny lives.

All the hope and excitement they'd held so carefully in their hands, their oh-so-fragile dreams, were broken, slipping from their grasp without a sound. And in their place was a grief so all-consuming, it felt like being turned inside out. Alice's joy in life was spilling all over the floor, all of its colour gone. She needed to get out, out of that room with its pain and its loss and the flood of grief that rushed through her veins. She stumbled through the door, filled with a kind of shame that she had dared to believe once again in her dream.

So stupid to think it could be hers.

Alice stumbled to the car, blinded by tears, while George finished paying for the private scan they had been so excited to book. Sitting in the passenger seat of the car, Alice's emotions overwhelmed her, and her heart broke, excruciating sobs wrenching from her gut as the torment of grief split her in two. As George returned to the car, she hunched around her aching body, unable to look at him or speak, desperate to get home.

It had been too good to be true, and now the twins she'd only just dared to imagine, the most beautiful gift from their incredible European summer adventure, were gone.

Her empty belly now bore the bruises of injections, the stretchmarks of hormone-induced weight gain, and her breasts were tender from the progesterone and oestrogen pills she'd been taking on and off for months now. Body confidence no longer existed.

Scanning the local leisure centre's class timetable the day before, she'd decided against the high-impact aerobic classes and opted instead for the gentler choice of yoga. 'I'm sure even in my unfit state, I can manage a bit of yoga!' she'd smiled weakly at George as they'd pottered around the kitchen making dinner.

But now, as she sat shyly facing the instructor, her reflection staring back at her in the floor-to-ceiling mirrors, Alice blushed at her beginner status amongst all these yoga-aficionados, and she began to lose the glimmer of confidence she'd summoned up, and wished she'd stayed at home.

Gradually though, the music and gentle encouragement of the instructor started to weave their magic, and Alice began to stretch and persuade her body into positions it hadn't held for a long time. Bit by bit, she felt her tired, achy muscles come back to life.

Holding poses and focusing on maintaining a slow, steady breath, Alice felt an inner confidence creep back to her, beginning to realise that her body was capable of more than being prodded, poked and berated for not being able to do what so many other women could without effort. Closing her eyes to be alone with her thoughts, Alice tried to believe something that she hadn't thought about herself for a very long time – that she was strong.

Alice enjoyed the feeling and tried to relax into the poses she was being taught. Then all too soon, the class was over. She followed suit as everyone lay down on their mats, closing their eyes, ready for the relaxation part of the class. The room fell quiet as the instructor led them through a guided meditation to music to slow their breathing and relax tired muscles.

The instructor's hypnotic voice over emotive swells of music initially calmed Alice, who closed her eyes and relaxed into the moment, feeling the satisfying aches and pains of the exertion in her arms and legs. She felt her limbs becoming heavy and her breathing slowing.

Later, she wouldn't be able to quite explain what happened in those quiet moments of reflection. Perhaps it was the connection with her body that she hadn't felt for a long time. Maybe it was the quiet, calm reflection that left her alone with her thoughts. Perhaps it was the powerful music that touched emotions she hadn't felt for years.

But all she knew at the time was that a frightening, sudden and previously unfamiliar sensation of emotional pain grew without warning as she lay quietly in the darkened room, lost in her thoughts. Sensory flashbacks, a sense of something dark and sinister, flooded her mind like ink, staining everything in its path and causing every hair on her body to stand on end.

In hindsight, she may have realised that the hypnotic power of the music had prised open a firmly shut box of trauma inside her mind, and it was that that was triggered, causing her to jerk upright, heart pounding, as unwelcome images crowded her thoughts. But at the time, she couldn't understand the panic that overwhelmed her, the urge to move, the desperate instinct to run and escape that overpowered her so completely. The sweaty palms and racing heart that told her she was in danger.

Alice ran from the class, ignoring the instructor's concerned calls, and never looked back, gulping in desperate, panicky breaths as she emerged into the too-bright sunlight of the day.

NOW

After a challenging few weeks, George had taken a day off work to support Alice and Tegan. Hearing him getting up and moving around downstairs that morning, Alice opened her eyes and pushed herself up slowly into a seated position against the cushions in the bed. She hadn't slept well, woken up several times by the sudden screams of Tegan's night terrors and struggling to fall asleep once it fell quiet, her nerves on edge. Her eyes were sore and her head was heavy. She could hear George on the stairs and smiled as she saw him come into the bedroom bearing a cup of steaming hot tea. Her smile quickly faded as she immediately noticed that something was wrong, her heart rate picking up straightaway.

'What's the matter, what's happened?' she burst out. Looking at George, she could see that whatever it was had shaken him, it was written all over his face. He was white, all colour drained from him, and his usually strong and steady voice shook slightly as he spoke.

'It's Tegan. Something's really wrong, and I just don't know what to do.'

George explained to Alice how he'd heard banging noises coming from Tegan's bedroom early that morning. So, he'd knocked on her door and then opened it to see if she was okay, but she wasn't.

'Tegan was sitting in the window,' he said, his voice choking up as he went on to explain. 'Her hands and face were smeared with blood – she must have cut herself then rubbed it on her face. She was pressing her face and hands against the glass, banging on it, screaming, shouting "help", trying to get the attention of the passers-by on the street below.'

At this, George sat on the side of the bed and hung his head in his hands. 'She turned and looked at me, and there was so much anger in her face. She shouted at me to get out of her room. I asked her to wash her face and hands, please get dressed and come downstairs and then just left her for a few minutes.'.

'Where is she now?' asked Alice, finding it hard to suppress the panic that was threatening to overwhelm her at this new and worrying development. Self-harm, a frightening new behaviour that they had no idea how to tackle.

'She's downstairs. After five minutes, she came downstairs, fully dressed, smiling, and asking for her breakfast as if nothing had happened. I've cleaned her up, dressed the cut on her hand, given her coco pops and settled her on the sofa in front of the television. She's got her teddy and weighted blanket.'

George looked at Alice, despair creeping into his expression. 'She's five years old, Alice. She's only a little girl and she's hurting so much. Whatever it is that she's seen or experienced just feels so huge, beyond our capabilities as parents.' He paused. 'I'm worried. I just don't know how to help her, and I feel like we're out of our depth here. I'm scared – what if she makes allegations against us? What are people going to think if they see her covered in blood, screaming, and shouting help from her bedroom window?

I just don't know what we can do.

We need help, and we need it soon.'

Sami

NOW

It's late when Sami rushes through the doors of the maternity ward. Night has fallen like a heavy curtain outside. The automatic doors of the hospital close and a hush surrounds Sami. Like a mother who settles a child to sleep, the ward's reverent calm slows her steps and quietens her harried mind. The wards are lit softly, with a quiet bustle of nurses patrolling the halls.

Sami had just opened a cold beer and taken a sip when the call came in. Most evenings she works late, writing up case notes, hunched uncomfortably over the tiny desk in the corner of her flat's small living space. Lit by a single light.

Her eyes itch, a headache rumbling at her temples. It has been a long, frustrating week. Stretching out, she yawns and pads to the kitchenette in her socks.

It was her manager on the phone.

'It's Piper. She's asking for you – he's here. The baby. Five hours old!'

Not going was out of the question. Now, Sami takes a deep breath and sanitises her hands again. Hungry, plaintive cries pierce the air as tiny babies claim their place in the world. Demanding attention.

Sami imagines their indignant faces being cradled, shushed and smooshed by loved-up new mums, bleary-eyed from lack of sleep, high on oxytocin. She feels a pang of something she can't identify, and pushes it away.

For Sami, a trip to a maternity ward is often a reluctant one, emotional and fraught with difficulties. The hardest job in the world. It means a new baby is born. Innocent and new, unaware of the mess it is born into. Suddenly seized from its mother, then straight to foster care, to new parents and a new life.

But this time, she is emotional for a different reason. She's here to see Piper. The most fragile of new parents. Her fragility evident in the way that she has no one visit but the social worker on the first day of her son's precious life. Delicate and still scarred from losing her first baby, Piper clings tightly to her newest child.

Due to Piper's history, she needs to have social worker involvement. Her new baby will be monitored closely until they can guarantee he is well cared for. A supervision order will likely remain in place until at least his first birthday. Social services are, understandably, twitchy about new babies going home with mothers whose first babies have been neglected. A three-year-old might survive on little food for a short while, but a new-born would not.

Sami thinks back to that critical meeting when she fought for Piper to keep her son. Sami laid out all the evidence she'd gathered, advocating passionately for a woman who had no voice but hers. The weight of responsibility for this tiny new life sits heavily on Sami's shoulders.

Piper must be tired, but the rapture of childbirth can be read in her eyes. They're bright and dancing with a fierce love. The baby at her mottled breast plump and pink, encased by Piper's hands that hold him firm and strong. She looks at Sami with the expression of a woman primed for survival.

'How are you doing?' Sami whispers. 'Hey little guy, hi, welcome to the world, baby!' Pulling up a seat, Sami sits at a distance from Piper and the baby, and resisting the urge to coo over the tiny new-born, asks all the questions her job requires, as well as offering Piper some much needed reassurance. The new mum answers all the questions softly, never taking her eyes off the tiny nursling clinging firmly onto her thumb with his strong grip.

When it is time to go, Sami gets up and wishes Piper well. She reminds her that she'll be visiting as soon as Piper and the baby are home, and to keep up with health visitor appointments. To get it right this time. To keep this tiny boy close. Safe. To nourish and nurture him. To give him a chance.

I'm on your side, Piper, Sami thinks quietly.

She turns at the door when Piper, her voice confident and strong, calls her name. She has a voice at last, and now she will use it. Ferocious love for her babies makes her strong. The hospital gown slips down over her shoulder, revealing a tattoo. The creamy skin across her heart is boldly marked: *Tegan.*

Her message is unmistakable. I'm back, and I'm prepared to fight. Whatever it takes.

'I want her back, Sami. I want Tegan back with me.'

Alice

NOW

On days when she retreated back under the duvet before 9:00 a.m., Alice felt like a flawed superhero displaced to the dark side.

As a prospective adopter going through the assessment process, you feel good, Alice thought. Learning about trauma, driven to help a child from a complicated past, working through often-invasive assessments. You're filled with self-worth, reinforced by assessors, friends and family. You're doing something good, your friends tell you. Your references are excellent, the social workers say. It's exciting.

Driven to make a difference, to do something great, you set out to change a young person's life. The training is hard, but it feels productive, purposeful.

But once the small stranger is home and they don't bond with you, you're on your own. Good feelings are replaced with those of failure. Why can't I love this child? Why do they hate me so much? When will the rages stop?

Huddled under blankets in a pit of something a lot like shame, Alice would open her social medias and lose hours to mindless scrolling. Trying to numb the endless whirring of her anxious mind.

But these days, she could no longer face looking at happy mummy accounts. Her stomach filled with a deep sadness every time she was reminded of how hopeful they'd been at the beginning of their journey. Even the new adopter accounts she'd gobbled up so eagerly in the early days of their journey were too much for her right now.

Seeing adoption announcements, filled with so much excitement and joy, broke Alice's heart almost as entirely as pregnancy announcements always had before.

Instead, she found herself searching for different hashtags. Her most commonly searched tags now were #adoptionbreakdown and #adoptiondisruption. She felt dirty, as though she were a teenager, skipping school, hiding behind the bike sheds to consume forbidden substances.

Here she was, a mum at last to a beautiful little girl, yet she was hiding away, reading stories of breakdown and loss. On those sites, she found tales that broke her heart. Lurking on a group for those whose adoptions had failed, whose children had returned to live in care, felt like the most appropriate home for her online.

She read and read, even though the stories she found there terrified her.

The first time she did it, she was shocked. Alice had always believed that if things went wrong with the adoption, or if they struggled, the team around the child, the social workers who had placed Tegan, would be there for them with kindness and understanding. But the more she read, the more she began to doubt this firmly held belief. Horror gradually built up in her chest when she realised it might not be the case – that if they needed help, the support they asked for might not be as forthcoming as she'd hoped.

Alice read, wide-eyed, stories of families who had been persecuted by social services. Ordinary, kind people dragged through court hearings that blamed their parenting after failing to cope with their adopted children's complex and extreme behavioural needs.

Alice's heart would be in her throat as she read post after post of families struggling with stories often so heartbreakingly similar. A child, usually older, fails to attach after years of worsening aggression, anger, trauma, and destruction.

The parents, desperate, seeking help and finding none. Support that is promised but never materialises. Exclusions from school. Parental depression, anxiety, and a growing sense of helplessness unfolds like a horror story as Alice reads on, not wanting to read anymore but unable to pull herself away. The details are compulsive, breaking Alice's heart but also providing her with some sense of safety, of familiarity all the same.

She reads about children running away from home, threatening their parents with violence. Families and lives torn apart. The child returned to the state's care, and the parents blamed and blacklisted by the social services charged with these children's care. Responsible for the well-being of adoptive families.

Parents left suffering with often lifelong feelings of guilt and shame, made worse by often being accompanied by a lack of understanding from family members and friends. Poor mental and physical health from being subjected to years of abuse both from their children and the social services meant to protect them. Blaming the adoptive parents because if they didn't, they'd have to re-examine the whole system that allowed these failures to happen in the first place.

Alice didn't talk to George about what she'd read. She tried not to let it affect how she related to Tegan, as difficult as that was. She tried to put on a happy face, to be the mum she knew she needed to be, even though she was rejected by this small, scared girl every day.

Yet inside her, vibrations of fear and anxiety accompanied Alice in everything she did, as her worries snowballed. Every day when she woke up, they filled the cavity of her chest with their weight.

She thought of how Charlie ran after her, that horrible day at Adrian and Michael's house. Alice had rushed to the car, head down, wanting to hide and never see her prep group friends again. But as George strapped Tegan into her car seat, Charlie caught up with her and touched her arm, kindly.

'It's okay, Alice. I can see that you're finding things hard right now. It's okay. We all understand how hard it is. How relentless it can be. Please talk to us whenever you need to, okay? We're always here – all of us. Lean on us. I don't know how we can help, but we'd like to try.'

It had been too much. Alice turned away from her, trying not to cry, looking at Charlie through the car window getting smaller and smaller as George quietly drove them away, towards home. They didn't truly understand. How could they? The only people who really got it were those who'd been through it.

Becka

NOW

Becka was in her studio painting, rock music pounding from her earbuds, when the call came in. Inspired, she sang along to her favourite tunes, feeling an uplifting sensation of being young again, creative and free of responsibilities. What a feeling it was, brought on by the time, space and freedom to be creative, the swelling emotion of the music and the absence of her babies. Becka was in her element. The artist inside her reborn.

It was the first time Becka had worked on a new project since the babies had arrived, and she felt a strange mix of excitement and nerves as the first colours went on to the canvas. She was always confident of her abilities before, now she wondered if being a mum had stripped her of her creative edge. Well, I guess only the finished result will tell, she thought.

Earlier that morning, Charlie had dressed two wriggly boys in brightly coloured splash suits and wellies and set off for the park to play and feed the ducks. Before leaving the house, she'd brought a coffee and croissants upstairs to Becka, instructing her to relax, have a long lie-in, a bath, and some time to herself.

'Love you, gorgeous,' she'd said. 'Enjoy a morning of quiet! I'll keep them out as long as I can! Stay in bed. That's an order, okay?!'

Instead, on hearing the door click shut, Becka had pulled on some dungarees and impatiently pushed her hair up into a bun. Her long-neglected studio awaited her, and she couldn't wait to get started. Watching the boys play by the pond the day before, dressed in brightly coloured raincoats, Becka had an idea for a canvas. In her mind, it came to life: primary colours, two small children holding hands and facing away from the painter, the eddying swirls of water, the budding signs of spring representing the children's youth and innocence. Now, she was desperate for her ideas to flow seamlessly onto the canvas, like a child bursting with a story they just have to tell.

So immersed was Becka in her work and the music filling her ears that, at first, she didn't notice the ringing of her mobile phone on the table behind her. When she was working, she'd usually leave the phone in the house to not be disturbed. But such uncontactable luxuries had disappeared since she became a mother. She never knew when she may be needed, so these days, her phone never left her side.

Sitting down on the beanbag under the window, Becka's cat, Biscuit, purred insistently, pushing at her hand as she checked who'd called. The missed call had been from Patricia, the children's social worker for Parker and Phoenix. What could she want? Becka wondered. It wasn't time for the boys' next LAC review yet, and they'd received an email last week to say that the court paperwork was all in order. Unsure of the reason for the call, Becka felt her heart rate begin to pick up as she dialled Patricia back. Her anxiety raised even higher when the other woman picked up straight away after just one ring.

'Hi, Becka? It's Patricia. I hope you and the family are all okay. Listen, I won't beat around the bush, I've got some upsetting news. Are you somewhere where you can sit down? You're not driving or anything?'

'Umm, no, I'm here at home, I'm okay. What is it, Patricia? You're worrying me now! Is everything okay with the boy's adoption application and court?' At the sound of Patricia's concerned tones, Becka's heart had begun to race, and her palms were sweating. What could this bad news possibly be?

'Yes, that's all fine, it's just... well, it's Keira. I'm so sorry, Becka, but I'm ringing to say that Keira died yesterday.

They think it was an overdose, but they can't tell me much more at this stage.

'I know how much you had hoped to meet the boys' birth mother one day, so I can understand how much this must come as a shock to you. But I wanted to let you and Charlie know as soon as possible.'

And just like that, she was gone. Keira was gone. And Becka sat stock-still, quite unable to comprehend the sense of loss and shock she felt at the continuing tragedy of Keira's short life, now cut so very short. The one last link to her boys' birth family, the parent Becka had hoped they would one day meet and learn so much from, gone forever. Tears crept into Becka's eyes, and she wept for her sons, for all they'd lost, and for their first mother, whose life choices had given her so little opportunity to heal.

Adrian

THEN

As a child, Adrian never knew what to expect when he came home from school, and for good reason.

Some days, his house would be a beacon of fairy lights and balloons, his mum dancing on the front path, dressed as a rainbow, hair coloured pink, wanting to party. On those days, she'd kiss Adrian, declare him the best boy in the world, and the evening would be a celebration, meaning dinner was homemade fairy cakes and ice cream. But Adrian craved sausages and mash like the other kids in his class had for dinner.

His fabulous, beautiful mum would turn up the music in the living room and, more often than not, reveal with a 'ta-da!' a handful of his bemused classmates sitting, bedecked in party hats, in a line on the sofa, yelling 'surprise!' as he walked in.

'It's not your birthday, is it?' Matthew from next door whispered to him as they hid in the bathroom, eating contraband ham sandwiches, on a particularly extravagant 'just-because' day. Adrian shook his head, finding it too difficult to explain.

Adrian loved to see his mum happy, it was the contrast to the bad days that made his spirits soar when he saw her beautiful smile. And he might have enjoyed the impromptu parties more if he didn't know exactly how it would end. At first, it would be fun, like having a birthday every day. But as the evening went on, with friends leaving and Adrian's bedtime nearing, his mum's mania would spiral, forcing him to dance harder, sing louder and eat more as he tried to keep up. He would feel sick from her demands, and she would shout with frustration at his dullness.

Spinning in ever-increasing circles of motion, his mum would whizz around him, switching on radio, television and stereo until the house was a blur of noise and stimulation. But still, it wouldn't be enough. Adrian's father would arrive home from work later, ever later, and switch everything off. With a quiet and tender love, he would take his mum by the hand to bed, gently untangling brightly coloured streamers from her hair, and then tuck Adrian in when he remembered.

One of those nights, Adrian crept up to the bedroom when his dad was downstairs and cuddled in next to his mum. Her lipstick would be smudged, and her eyeliner shadowed her eyes. She had those beautifully sad eyes that could be bright, dancing and full of joy one day, but so dark and empty the next. As a child, Adrian would stroke the long, wavy hair that covered the pillow, and tuck his teddies in next to his sleeping mum, to keep her safe in the night.

The next day, the colour was gone, always gone. And instead of a song, freshly baked croissants and a kiss, silence met him where his much-loved mother had been. Adrian would get himself up, dressed and to school. The house, on his return, would be dark, with his mother still in bed and dinner in the freezer.

His teenage years continued like this with very little change, a loving but absent father and unpredictable mother, until Adrian went to college. There he met his first boyfriend and, finding his mother in between mania and depression one day, he decided it would be a good time to come out as they sat with cups of tea in the lounge. Met with tight hugs and understanding, he held his mother close, and he wept at the genuine moment of connection with the wonderful woman he loved and had missed for so long.

Encouraged by this, he brought his boyfriend home to meet her to find a banner across the front of the house declaring *'Congratulations!'* in giant letters, a Pride flag on the door, and music blaring from the speakers in the lounge windows for the whole neighbourhood to hear. His mother, as his father whispered when he greeted them at the door, was teetering on the edge of collapse.

'Let's go,' Adrian said quietly to his first boyfriend, not quite knowing how the meeting of this fledgling relationship and his manic mother would go.

But creeping down the garden path, the anguished screams of his mother's voice still reached him as he left, accusing him of things he'd never even read about in magazines, as his boyfriend flushed red in the face and couldn't look him in the eye.

After that, Adrian knew that all the love in the world couldn't change it. He started to protect his heart, bidding a gentle 'goodbye' and a 'stay strong' to his father. Packing his things, Adrian moved in with his boyfriend's family.

His boyfriend's parents liked things to stay the same, eating something-and-chips and drinking strong tea in front of *Coronation Street* each night. Adrian liked this predictability of everyday family life a little too much after what he'd come from. It led his boyfriend to despair, begging Adrian to rebel, to get off the sofa and go out with their friends like all the other eighteen-year-olds they knew.

The relationship didn't last. His boyfriend moved away to university, and Adrian got a job and found a flat of his own, but their brief time together showed Adrian what he wanted, although he wasn't sure how he'd get there.

Adrian wanted a safe and settled life with a husband, and a love that would be constant and true. A comfortable, drama-free life. A dog, a cat, a husband, a job and a home would be everything he could ever wish for and more.

Alice

NOW

The front door clicked closed, and Cara left Alice and George's house after completing her final individual assessment with Alice, an emotional session that left both women with tears in their eyes.

On saying goodbye, Cara had clasped Alice's hand and said quietly, 'Well done, Alice. Thank you for being so honest with me. It's been an honour to sit with you as you've told your story, and I just wanted to say thank you for trusting me.' And with that, she left, promising to check in soon, and Alice turned to her husband, who was back downstairs, offering a hug.

Taking George's hand, Alice said quietly, 'I think we need to talk.'

Sitting across from George in the kitchen, coffee in hand, she knew it was time to be painfully honest about the life with Axel she'd only ever glossed over before. Feeling heartbroken at what she was about to tell him, and looking into her husband's loving gaze, Alice began.

After working with Cara, her voice no longer shook when she told her story. Now it was unwavering as she confidently spoke her truth, clasping George's strong hands tight in hers, knowing it would be just as hard for him to hear as it would be for her to tell.

'I told you about Axel before, but I haven't been entirely honest with you about what happened when I left him.

'It's tough because I'll never know exactly what happened that night, and there's no way now of remembering what they did. But what I do know is that they did something to me, something irreparable. They took something from me that night that I can never get back, and

I need you to know that I struggle with that knowledge every day.

'The day I left Axel and moved into my flat was the most significant step I've ever had to take in my life. You have to understand how young I was then, how much I trusted him, even when it became abundantly clear that he wasn't the person I thought he was. He hurt me beyond words, but it didn't happen overnight. At first, it was beautiful. Flowers, chocolates, nights out and parties, meeting new people every night. He took me to places I'd never been before – gallery openings, museums, the best table in a nice restaurant. I had no idea how he could get those things; he was only a bar manager in a hotel, but he did. At first, and I know it's a cliché, but he swept me off my feet.

'Leaving him was frightening, but even then, I knew that staying with someone who hit and insulted me every day was more terrifying than starting again on my own.

'On the first day in my new flat, I spent every minute jumping at every noise I heard, looking over my shoulder every time a floorboard creaked, my heart racing, waiting for him to come home, and the abuse to start all over again. I was just waiting for him to hit me again.

'It took time, but slowly I got stronger. Though, I was still scared to meet new people and make new friends. After everything that Axel had done to me, my confidence was at rock bottom and socialising terrified me. I know it sounds crazy to say that somehow going back to Axel felt safe, and I always swore to myself before that I'd never do it, but that night he invited me to the party was a weak point. Alone in my flat, with no friends to call and no one to turn to, I was lonely and frightened. And then he turned up on the doorstep, charming as ever, and all I wanted to do was believe that he'd changed.

'In hindsight, I realise this was no ordinary party, and he was no ordinary man. He was sick, and this was a revenge attack. It's taken me many years to be able to say this out loud, to acknowledge the horror of it. To no longer feel the sickness, shame and disgust run through my whole body at the realisation of how deliberate and evil it was. He planned it, and I had no idea.

'Afterwards, I tried to get on with my life. I was so embarrassed, ashamed, and felt like it was my fault. I didn't dare trust anyone with what had happened, and anyway, I couldn't remember it. I thought no one would believe me because I couldn't remember any details of the night, but I knew something awful had happened.

'Years later, I went to the gym. It was after our last IVF attempt, do you remember? I wanted to start feeling like myself again, feeling healthier, fitter. But something changed that day – the music, the way I moved parts of my body in ways I hadn't done before – I don't know what it was, but it triggered me, and after all that time, the flashbacks began. So many long-forgotten emotions raced up to the surface, it was a trauma that needed to be healed.

'Everything was shadowy and confused. I'd lie awake at night, unable to sleep because every time I closed my eyes, I saw mocking, laughing faces leering at me from the shadows. The horrible sensation of my body being pulled, pushed and stretched in every direction. Hands all over me. My head hurt from trying to piece it all together, and I'd cry because I knew the drugs from that night kept me from remembering what happened. But gradually, I began to become aware that my body had kept the score. And the pain was in there, somewhere.

'Bit by bit, I began to recall some of that night. The way my consciousness had slipped away so quickly, the feeling of rough hands grabbing me, hands that weren't Axel's, the feeling of falling painfully to the ground. Then waking up, like a discarded doll, thrown onto a pile of coats. Groggy, my head pounding and my whole body in pain.

'They raped me, George.

'It's taken me a long time to dare to say that word, and even now, it hurts me to say it. Even though I don't remember it consciously, something deep within me knows beyond doubt that it happened.

'It wasn't just one man, and it wasn't just once.

'They hurt me, and that's why we can't get pregnant. That's why I can never give you a baby. And trust me when I say that I have regretted what happened that night every single day of my life.

'George, they took everything from me. But I need you to know that you, and the family we may be about to have, mean everything to me now. And I couldn't bear it if any of this pain from my past hurt our precious, lovely future.'

And with that, Alice and George clasped hands. He didn't say anything because he didn't need to. The adoption assessment process had brought them so much more examination of their pasts than they had ever anticipated, and now they sat together as they quietly acknowledged the depth of the pain they'd just shared. Holding each other tight, they felt closer than ever and more ready than before to move forward with their plans for a family, strong and united.

Piper

THEN

Rock bottom looks different for everyone. For some, it's an intervention. One drink too many, leading to an accident when drunk. An angry outburst that ends a friendship forever. A misunderstanding over money. Rock bottom is painful however it comes about.

But what rock bottoms all have in common is the sense that life needs to change. That things can't go on like this.

Piper's rock bottom came the day she dropped her daughter off at nursery with no idea how the little girl had got herself dressed that day, only to receive a telephone call just one hour later.

'It's Tegan. She's had a wee accident, and we don't have any clean clothes for her. And, um, she wasn't wearing any underwear today. Would it be okay if we dressed her in something from the spare clothes box?'

The kindly nursery manager assured Piper that it wasn't a problem, that they'd take care of it. That she didn't need to worry about washing or returning the clothes, and they hoped that everything was okay at home.

The question was a trigger for Piper, and, angry at barely being able to answer the woman's gently posed questions, she muttered something about picking Tegan up early that day and put the phone down.

Her head had hurt that morning, heavy from the vodka she'd consumed the night before, and the nursery run had passed by in a blur. Picking up her child later, Piper realised that not only was her little girl dressed in someone else's clothes, but she also wasn't wearing a coat in the middle of November.

Telling herself that it didn't matter, Piper reminded herself that all mums made mistakes, it was just part of being a mum. No one got it right all of the time. The most important thing was that Tegan was wanted and well-loved. And, anyway, Piper thought of the way the child had skipped happily towards her when she arrived at nursery pick-up. Tegan had jumped into her arms for a cuddle, shouting 'Mummy!'. That was the only proof she needed that she was doing a good job.

With this thought in mind, Piper cuddled up with Tegan in her bed that afternoon, feeding the girl chocolate and crisps. It was the warmest place in the house as she'd run out of money for the electricity meter. She told her it was their little treat as they watched back-to-back episodes of *Peppa Pig* on Piper's phone.

'It's lovely being cuddled up together with Mummy, in Mummy's bed, isn't it, darling?' she'd said, holding on tight to her girl, stroking her hair.

'It is Mummy. I love it. It's much nicer than my bed. I love you, Mummy.'

Piper didn't think anything of it at the time. Sleepily she settled down in bed, enjoying the cosy feeling of being cuddled up with her little girl – the two of them against the world. The house was safe, quiet and calm now that Ryan, and his temper, had left them. They might not have any money, and their house might be a bit grubby, but they were together. They'd make it through.

It wasn't until later, when Tegan had fallen asleep in her bed, that Piper wondered what she'd meant about her bed not being as cosy as Piper's. Easing herself out carefully from underneath her daughter's sleeping body, Piper crossed the hall into Tegan's bedroom.

Pulling back the tangled mess of bedcovers, teddies and blankets, Piper put her hand over her mouth at the sudden foul smell that hit her. Tucked underneath the bedclothes was a pile of faeces, smeared over the duvet and sheets, staining Tegan's favourite teddy. Even her comfort blanket – the one she sucked to help her to sleep at night – hadn't escaped untouched, and to make it worse, there was a bad-smelling wet patch at the bottom of the bed. Piper had no idea whether it was spilled juice or the urine of her two-year-old daughter. She had no recollection of the last time she'd changed her daughter's bedclothes or even pulled the covers back far enough to see what could be hidden underneath.

Piper gagged, the sight and smell of her tiny daughter's bed turning her stomach. Shame and horror of how she could have let herself and her daughter find themselves in this situation engulfed her, and she could barely bring herself to touch the bed to clean it. She felt a sudden, uncontrollable feeling of anger rush through her. An animal wail of distress pushed its way up from her gut to her mouth as she cried and cried, hands over her face as she slid helpless to the floor.

When the social workers wrote up their case notes later, they explained their reasons for removing Tegan from Piper's home. The report detailed how the house was so neglected that the social workers assigned to the job struggled to believe that the house was inhabited when they first visited, listening to the wind whistling around the unheated living room from a broken window pane at the front of the house. None of the sofas or chairs were clean enough to sit on, dirt saturated the living room carpet, and rat droppings could be found on kitchen worktops.

One health visitor left the house after a visit and had to stumble around the corner to cry, devastated by the thought that a mother and child had been living in such squalor.

The assessor's notes talked about how Tegan's feet and legs were always dirty and red raw with flea bites, and that she often went to nursery having got herself ready. She smelled of urine and sweat, and it was hard to tell when she may have last been bathed. Often dressed in inappropriate clothing that was still damp or smelling slightly of mildew, having been left at the bottom of the washing machine, it was also noted that Tegan did not own a warm coat, hat or gloves in the winter, and she was always desperately thin and hungry, stealing leftovers from her friends' plates or out of the bin before the nursery staff noticed what was happening and served up double helpings of everything to Tegan from then on.

The social workers talked about having insufficient evidence to remove the child but that their concerns escalated every time they visited.

Then there came a day when they finally judged the bar to have been reached, and the neglect was severe enough for removal. On that day, they collected Tegan from nursery. She had just turned three. She was dressed in thin, grubby summer clothes, and her hair was matted with dirt.

They strapped her safely into a car seat in the back of the car and drove her away to a place where she'd be fed and kept safe. She cried and screamed all the way there. Kicking her feet and hitting her dirty little hands on the glass as the social worker in the back of the car tried to calm her down. But nothing could stop the screaming. The little girl wailed and cried, screaming for her mummy to come back.

Adrian

THEN

'Hello, Ruby love. How are you doing today? Come on in, sit down there, that's it. I'll get you a cup of tea.'

Settling the woman at her favourite table in the corner next to the craft supplies — her daughter's preferred activity – Marjorie headed back towards Adrian and Michael shaking her head gently in a message they understood all too clearly.

'She's not having such a good day today, poor love,' she said quietly, busying herself brewing two strong cups of tea, four sugars in each, popping a custard cream on the edge of each saucer.

It was early on a Saturday morning, and the centre was quiet, the air still warming through as the gently humming wall heaters woke up. Chairs were placed in small groups at tables or near the toy boxes, encouraging parents to play and engage with their children, a selection of books featuring dinosaurs set up on the side, accompanied by a couple of plastic brontosauruses.

The contact centre staff's mission was to encourage play, connection, and meaningful experiences for the children and adults who used the centre, and they worked hard to create an environment that would support that.

For children without toys at home, it might be one of the only opportunities they had to freely explore a toy box and experience what other children did every day. Adrian kept this in mind as he did his final checks of the room, placing a cuddly teddy bear in the chair next to Ruby, knowing her six-year-old daughter would love it. Ruby, her head buried in her phone, forehead creased in a frown, didn't even look up.

That morning, Adrian and Michael had arrived at 8:30 a.m. to work with Marjorie to get the centre ready for its guests – tacking safeguarding posters to the wall, setting up the front desk with its signing in book, and remembering to turn on the water heater for those all-important teas and coffees.

Today, Michael would work in the canteen, taking money and handing out drinks and snacks, and Adrian would sit at the front desk with Marjorie, taking telephone calls, signing people in and answering queries, all the time accompanied by the dulcet tones of the church choir which met in the basement to rehearse at the same time every week.

They didn't open the doors officially until 9:00 a.m. but, having volunteered at the centre for many years, Marjorie knew Ruby well enough to know that the woman travelled across the city, taking three buses, navigating public transport with a bad leg and a walking stick just to get there. In Marjorie's book, if a woman was prepared to do that to see her child, she wasn't going to turn her away.

Charlie had suggested that Adrian and Michael volunteer at the centre after the topic came up in conversation one day. Seeking childcare experience and knowledge of the issues around fostering and adoption before going to the approval panel, the two men approached Charlie for suggestions in her capacity as a former social worker. The child contact centre was the perfect solution.

Set up to facilitate contact between children and their non-custodial parents, child contact centres ran across the country on a Saturday morning and were solely staffed by volunteers. Many children who attended were at risk of being removed from their families to be fostered or adopted, and many of the families were known to social services.

Affected by drugs, alcoholism, mental and physical illness, poverty and domestic abuse, the reasons for parents not living with their children were wide-ranging, as well as heart-breaking. Often separated partners could not agree on contact. That was when the contact centre stepped in, mandated by family courts to facilitate safe, regular communication between the parents and child. Other times, grandparents had custody of children not able to be cared for by their parents. These children were often the luckier ones – well-groomed, happy and safe – brought to the contact centre with prompt regularity by vigilant grandparents doing the best they could.

Keen to learn more about the issues affecting families at risk of losing their child to adoption, and gain a more profound empathy for birth families, Adrian and Michael enquired and were quickly approved. Once their DBS (Disclosure and Barring Service) checks came back clear, the centre manager welcomed the two men with open arms, telling them with a smile that they'd been crying out for new volunteers.

On their first day arriving at the church hall, they were shown the ropes by two women, both long-serving volunteers and members of the church, and quickly got up to speed. Since then, they'd enjoyed the work, getting to know the centre's regular users and the gossipy chats they had with Marjorie over cups of tea when it was quiet.

With everything set up and ready to go, Adrian and Michael sat in the small kitchen to have a quick cup of tea before the hectic morning began. Once the doors opened, it would be a rush to get everyone signed in and settled with their family members. There was always someone who forgot to sign the book, a child who ran off between someone's legs, or an absent family member they needed to call. And everyone always arrived at once. So, this would be the only chance they had to grab a quiet cuppa before it got busy.

'You know,' mused Adrian. 'Ruby really reminds me of my mum sometimes. I really hope she gets to see her daughter today.'

'I don't know whether she will,' replied Michael, sadly. 'You remember the way it went last week? Her daughter was scared, bless her. I empathise with both of them – it's horrible for it to end that way. And I can understand how she reminds you of your mum, love. It must be hard for you to see.'

The week before, Ruby had clearly been in the grips of an uncontrolled manic episode, arriving in a red dress, heels and feather boa, with her smile wide as she grabbed her bewildered six-year-old daughter, running around and laughing. She picked her up, swung her around and tickled her, the very picture of playfulness, but her exuberance was excessive, and her laugh too loud. Her behaviour was far too rowdy for the subdued coffee room where parents sat quietly playing with their children, and far too intense for her sensitive daughter, who loved colouring, drawing and reading. The daughter who had shyly shown the book she was reading about nature to Adrian when she'd arrived holding her grandmother's hand half an hour before.

'I'll show it to Mummy,' she'd said.

Not their place to intervene, Adrian and Michael had looked on sadly while Ruby's daughter had ended up sobbing on her grandmother's knee, refusing to talk to her mother, whose smile disappeared as quickly as it had arrived, and who wandered around the room aimlessly, chatting to anyone else who'd listen. The daughter soon left with her grandmother and Ruby sat in the corner, all exuberance gone, nursing a coffee for her allotted twenty minutes to ensure she didn't follow her daughter out of the building. When the time was up, she came to the desk to sign out. Adrian and Michael had had some good chats with Ruby when she'd been lucid and well, and she'd inquired kindly about their plans to adopt. Signing her name and the time in the book, she put down the pen and suddenly grabbed Adrian's arm, looking him directly in the eyes.

'When you get your child,' she whispered, 'you never let them go, you hear me? You hold onto that child and keep them close. Because once you let them go, you never get them back. Keep them close, you hear me?'

Now, putting down their coffees, Adrian and Michael made a point of keeping an eye out for Ruby that morning, to see if there was anything they could do to help. Looking at the woman now slumped listlessly in the corner, it was hard to imagine she was the flamboyant creature they'd seen the week before, but that was the nature of the illness, thought Adrian, his heart going out to this woman and her child.

He didn't have long to dwell on it though, as his attention was soon grabbed by shouting coming from the front desk. The door had been opened, and the centre users were beginning to arrive. He left the kitchen to see where the noise was coming from.

A woman was screaming at Marjorie, her hand gripping tightly onto Marjorie's arm as the older woman placed a gentle hand on the her back. Tears were pouring down her cheeks as she cried to anyone who'd listen.

'He says I can't see them, that he's not bringing them. He's not letting me see my kids. All because I missed one session. He's not bringing them. He's taking them out to see his new girlfriend instead. They're *my* kids. Call him, tell him he needs to be here, call the police!'

And so, the morning began.

Becka

NOW

Parker and Phoenix toddled happily around the garden, their delighted giggles sending a rush of love to Becka's heart. It was a fresh spring day, daffodils poking yellow heads out of buds and a rainfall of blossom floating over the fence on the breeze from their neighbour's mature cherry tree. The one holding the rope swing on its heavy boughs. The one the grandchildren fought over every summer, joy and squabbles filling the air. Happy memories, Becka thought.

Charlie called Becka over. 'Are you ready?' They were about to plant their own family cherry tree, and Becka was dreaming of similar happy memories to be made by their boys beneath its soft, pink canopy as they grew.

It had been an emotional time for the family since Patricia's call the week before. Patricia had asked Charlie and Becka if they wanted to attend Keira's funeral. There was no expectation they would go, but she wanted to give them the opportunity. Her funeral would be limited to a small number of family and friends, but given Keira had only a few of those, Charlie and Becka would be welcome.

Once Parker and Phoenix were in bed, Becka passed the news on to Charlie and asked her what she thought.

'I don't know,' came her response. 'If you want to go, we'll go. I understand why you feel the need to go. But I have concerns about our safety and that of the boys. There will be birth family members there, and we don't have anyone who can look after the boys on the day. I don't feel comfortable taking them. Yes, I'd like for us to pay our respects – and it would be nice to learn more about this woman who gave us our sons, and this is the last opportunity to do so – but it doesn't feel safe to me.'

And so, the two women agreed that they would pay their respects to Keira in their own way. Mourning the loss of their children's birth parent was not something that they'd been prepared for in their adoption assessments, and Becka and Charlie felt the gravity and responsibility of getting this right, not just for them but for their boys to learn about in the future.

Life story work was an essential element of any adopted child's experience. Parker and Phoenix were too young to understand their past right now, but Becka and Charlie knew that as they grew, it would be vital for them to be told why they were adopted in an age-appropriate way. Long gone were the days where children didn't find out they were adopted until they were adults. Now the advice was to weave stories about adoption into the child's experience as soon as they were able to understand. To ensure that the adopted child grew up with an awareness of their story.

Knowing this, Becka and Charlie had filled the playroom shelves with a diverse range of books featuring adopted children with different family make-ups – those with a mum and a dad, those with two mums or two dads, and those still looking for a family. They hoped that these stories would ensure that their boys never grew up wondering why they didn't live with their birth family and not knowing who to go to for answers.

Both boys had life story books featuring Becka, Charlie, their pets, and pictures of Keira. Patricia put these books together on the occasion of the boys moving to their new home. Offering precious details such as the boys' birth weight, their time of their birth, and happy memories of their time in foster care. These books would provide the boys with important context about their past as they grew.

The funeral day arrived, and Becka and Charlie knew they had to mark the day, so they decided to spend it as a cosy family day at home. Holding their sons on their knees, together on the sofa, they looked through the life story books together, pointing out pictures of Keira and telling the boys about her.

After much discussion, they decided to plant a tree in the garden in memory of Keira. Becka imagined the tree growing tall and strong as the boys did too, blossoming, thriving and one day sheltering them beneath it as they carved their initials in its trunk. With this in mind, Charlie went to the garden centre and selected a cherry tree, the blossom being Becka's favourite sight in spring. Bundling the boys up in splash suits and wellies, the family took to the garden to plant it, the children running around as Charlie prepared the earth.

Finally, it was time to lower the fledgeling tree into its new home. After patting down the soft earth around it, both women took a twin in their arms and said a silent prayer, reflecting on the troubled life of the young woman who had given them the ultimate gift, their beautiful boys. Looking at them now, Becka felt a fierce maternal instinct knowing she and Charlie were everything these boys had now.

'We'll look after them for you, Keira,' she whispered.

And at that moment, it was as if she fully stepped firmly into her protective role for these children, knowing she and Charlie were the only ones in the world for their boys. And despite her grief and sadness about their loss, it felt somehow safer now, knowing there was no competition out there for their love.

Adrian

THEN

'Maybe one day someone will break through that heart of stone you have in there, but it won't be me!' Noah yelled, slamming the door on his way out of Adrian's life, an overflowing bag spilling socks onto the floor as he slung it over his shoulder.

Adrian picked up the red socks, which were a Christmas present, paired them into a ball and put them away in a drawer before washing and drying the coffee cups on the table. Plumping up the cushions on the sofa and turning on the television, he was satisfied the flat was clean enough for him to start his weekend, a well-planned schedule of friends, gym workout, swim and relaxation.

Just how he liked it.

He'd moved into the modern city centre apartment a year before, excited to begin his new job with the prestigious law firm just a short walk away. After leaving university, he'd worked long hours, starting early and coming home late, not caring that he lived in flat shares as he was rarely home. But finding this job and flat after five years of work to get here felt like an accomplishment.

And he wasn't going to let anything get in his way.

An attractive man and confident in his sexuality, Adrian never had any problems meeting men and had had a string of partners since moving out of his boyfriend's parents' home at eighteen. Noah was the latest in a line of beautiful men with whom Adrian had enjoyed gourmet meals, excellent restaurants, cocktails, and a social life he'd only ever dreamed of.

Socialising came easily to Adrian, too. Leaving work on a Friday night, he was never happier than when he could head straight to a bar to meet up with a group of friends, de-stress from his week and wind down with a drink or two. Adrian had learned to be the life and soul of the party early on in his life, and it was a role he slipped into quickly within any group of friends. His mother's words, 'The party doesn't start till you walk in, my love!' rang perpetually in his ears, and Adrian knew he was popular and well-liked within his circle.

Stumbling home with Noah the night before, walking through the city lit up at night, Adrian had felt happy and high on life; a good job, great friends, a superb flat and a beautiful man on his arm. Growing up in his chaotic family, Adrian had wished for precisely this.

His expensive clothes, lavish lifestyle, and gruelling gym routine were all designed to reflect the luxurious lifestyle he worked so hard to cultivate.

Yes, his life was great.

Noah was wrong.

Adrian knew exactly what he wanted.

He loved what he loved and had many things he was passionate about.

Noah just wasn't one of them.

Alice

NOW

When it happened, it happened slowly, and then all of a sudden. Alice and George were not okay. They knew that much. They were barely paddling most days, but they were staying afloat.

'Of course, we're doing fine,' Alice had assured Tegan's headteacher the Monday morning after Tegan had had a particularly challenging week at school.

But inside, she was screaming.

And everything slowly fell apart.

Alice looked on helplessly as the careful and oh-so-delicate equilibrium they'd worked so hard to cultivate over the preceding months began to crumble.

Sami

NOW

Running past with a precarious pile of paperwork, Sami's boss slammed angrily into a meeting, sweeping up a couple of junior social workers on the way and closing them all into a meeting room as they scurried behind her.

The local authority office was busy that day, tempers were flaring, and workloads were toppling. Sami picked up on the underlying sense of stress as colleagues around her sighed impatiently, intermittently swearing when the phones started ringing, insistent, yet again.

'I haven't got time for this!' came a frustrated cry from the other side of the room.

It was one of those days. The workload was high, the cases were difficult, and a contagious sense of dissatisfaction crept like a virus through the office, infecting everyone in its wake. A new office junior, Sami forgets her name, ran crying into the ladies' toilets earlier after one too many harsh words from her boss. The rest of the staff, too busy to look up from their desks, hadn't noticed she was gone until the photocopier jammed and there was no-one there to fix it.

Now, looking through the glass meeting room window, Sami saw her boss slam her hand angrily on the table in front of her as she made a point. She looks like I feel, thought Sami, crossly. Sitting hunched over her computer, Sami was fuming.

Anger crept through every cell of her body as she readied herself to write up her notes and draft a letter to Alice and George. The meeting they'd had the night before had left her furious on Tegan's behalf and incapable of understanding what had gone wrong. As a child's social worker, she knew that the needs of the child were always put first. As far as Sami was concerned, this was the way it should be.

She had grown impatient as Alice had explained how difficult things had been for her lately. 'Well, how do you think Tegan feels?' she had interjected brusquely. Alice had looked at her sadly. Sami had no patience for her excuses.

So she was meant to believe now that a child who was chirpy, happy, chatty and friendly in foster care had suddenly become angry and dysregulated overnight? Impossible! Sami thought crossly back to the day she'd sat with Alice and George at their matching panel and advocated passionately for them to be Tegan's new parents. She'd believed in them. She'd fought for them. And now?

Now, they were telling Sami that they couldn't bond with this little girl, that they didn't feel the match was right. That Tegan's needs were too great. Sami gulped her coffee, the caffeine hit fuelling the righteous indignation she could feel buzzing in her veins. So, what, they just give up on her? On this girl who needs them more than anything? Sami was angry at herself for getting it so wrong, she could scream with frustration.

'Everything okay?' Sami's thoughts were interrupted as the admin manager's friendly enquiry reached her ears. The young woman was smiling at her kindly, and Sami realised as she straightened her face into a pleasant expression, just how deeply she'd been frowning while working.

'Yeah, all's okay. Thanks, Martha,' she replied. 'Just a tricky case. No change there!'

'Well, make an effort to get out in the sunshine at lunchtime, won't you? It's a beautiful day out there today!'

No chance of that, Sami grumbled to herself. She ran a hand through her hair and set to work. She would write a letter to Tegan's parents that clarifies the social services' opinion on the current situation, and it wouldn't be pretty. Yes, it's hard, but isn't that precisely what the training prepares them for?

Alice

NOW

With shaky hands, Alice let the offending letter fall to the floor, suddenly sickened to the pit of her stomach at what she'd read. It seemed her worst fears had come true, and she stood stock still, bent over slightly as if in pain. She felt herself becoming flooded with overwhelming emotions that were hard to contain.

Her cheeks flushed hot with indignity and disgust at the untruths contained in the letter. She recalled how it had dropped dangerously, like a concealed bomb, on their welcome mat that morning. Alice had been drinking her morning coffee, the stress of that morning's attempts at getting her daughter to school bringing on a headache that she'd just managed to tame with painkillers. Now it resurged, her blood thumping in her throat as she gulped back angry, horrified tears. Reading the letter, full of misinterpretations of everything they'd confided to Sami, Alice felt frozen in place, unsure of where to turn. Burning with a sense of prickling, horrifying shame.

They had arranged an emergency meeting with Sami last week, which had lasted three hours after Tegan had gone to bed. Alice and George had been assured that they'd been listened to, and Alice had felt as though a weight had been lifted from her shoulders. But now, she felt cheated, lied to, and let down. She felt the sense of anger resulting from being unjustly convicted, the shame of being labelled as a bad parent. There was a horror at having arrived in this situation. It felt so contrary to her life so far, one in which she was seen as a failure. A mother who couldn't mother her own child.

But Tegan wasn't her own child. Not really. Not yet. If she had been the birth child of Alice and George, she wouldn't have suffered like this. They wouldn't all be living this trauma. They wouldn't have found themselves in this impossible situation. Alice wouldn't be standing here, feeling like a criminal, in the hallway of her own home. She wouldn't be reading untruths about her and her husband written by the people she had been told she should trust.

The letter took everything they had painfully, haltingly told Sami and twisted it until it was barely recognisable. With the uncontrollable rages that they'd witnessed in Tegan portrayed as *'occasional temper tantrums'*, her worrying episodes of self-harm blamed on a *'lack of adequate parental supervision'* and Alice and George's attempts to parent this highly traumatised child described as an *'unwillingness to embrace therapeutic parenting'*.

An adoption support worker had once visited the house with Sami after Alice had been up all night without a wink of sleep with a screaming, night-terrored Tegan. This was portrayed as *'Alice did not engage with support'* and *'she did not make the worker feel welcome in her home'*.

Alice had just wanted to crawl into bed, feeling bone-tired and desperate for some real help for her child. Instead, she'd answered the door with a weak smile, made tea and brought biscuits. She'd listened to the adoption worker interrogate her repeatedly about her mental health, swerving any questions about what real support they could provide for Tegan.

What was all of this? Could this really be happening? Alice couldn't find sufficient words to explain how unjust it all was. They'd gone to Tegan's workers in good faith with a desperate cry for help, knowing this child deserved more than the limited support she'd been given. But instead of receiving adequate support, Alice and George were being portrayed as the ones to blame. The fact that she knew this awful letter had been written by Sami and her manager made it even worse. Who could she trust if she couldn't trust them?

If Alice had been thinking clearly – and she would look back on this with the clarity of hindsight – she may have questioned why the blame was falling so squarely at their door just months after the placement of a traumatised child.

She may have questioned why it was necessary to suggest that two highly organised, well prepared, well-recommended adopters were being vilified in this way.

Could it be that adoption wasn't right for this child? Could it be that the local authority made a mistake in placing her?

Becka and Adrian

NOW

Michael brought back coffees from the takeaway stand and handed two of them to Becka and Charlie, who took them gratefully.

'I need this,' Michael exclaimed, overjoyed that it was the end of the summer term. He was exhausted after balancing reports, school plays, and managing his staff. Combine this with having a child experiencing sleep regression, and Michael and Adrian were surviving on strong coffee and naps.

But today, it was the weekend and time to relax. The couples had met up at a local farm, and it was lovely for all of them to see the boys running free in front of them as the grown-ups chatted. They'd all been keen to catch up with each other's news since they'd last met.

Sipping her coffee, Charlie said, 'Just look at them!' marvelling at the fact that between the friends, they were parents to three such wonderful boys, running together as if they were all brothers, holding hands.

In the middle, Joey was not much bigger than the twins, his brown curls contrasting with their blond heads. All dressed in shorts, t-shirts, sandals and sunhats, slathered in sun lotion against the heat of the day, they looked so beautiful.

Just perfect, thought Becka.

It was the kind of family meet-up Becka and Charlie had dreamed of for so long, and they loved nothing more than seeing their boys make friends with other children. The sight of the three boys now, holding hands so sweetly, made Becka's heart sing.

It had been crucial to the two women that their sons have positive relationships with other adults and children. They knew how important it was for adopted children to have positive adult role models in their lives, and that the chances of healing from early life trauma were significantly improved by good relationships.

And having friends who had experienced a similar story, who were adopted, was essential to help the boys make sense of their stories. Making friends with Adrian and Michael's boy was easy and fun, a friendship that they hoped would last for a lifetime, and Becka and Charlie embraced Joey as if he were their own.

Sitting down on a bench, they watched as the children ran into the sandpit, eagerly heading for the buckets and spades.

'Gives us five minutes to drink our coffees!' said Charlie, smiling.

Adrian agreed. 'We were so sorry to hear your news about Keira. It must have come as such a shock?' he said, picking up a thread of conversation that had started earlier but been interrupted by the boys.

'It really was,' replied Becka. 'I don't know why I felt such a powerful mix of emotions when I heard the news. Although I didn't know her, I felt there would always be a connection between us, that I'd always think of her on certain occasions, the twins' birthdays, Christmas and Mother's Day, for example.

'She was their mother, she gave us our boys, she was their mum first, and I never want to forget that. I want to honour that, you know? We both hoped that the boys would have the chance to meet her, talk to her about their lives once they grew up. But now she's gone, and I can't stop thinking about her.

'Learning about her death, the overdose, it all felt like such a waste. The other day, I re-read the boys' child permanence report. It was as if I was reading it for the first time with fresh eyes, and all I could see was a life that was so difficult from the beginning, and it made me so sad. She hardly had a chance herself, and she was so young.

'It turns out that her parents were made bankrupt after some bad business decisions when she was just a little kid. Her dad slid slowly into alcoholism, her mum left them, and Keira ended up with a bad group of friends who pushed her towards drugs, skipping school, smoking, and bad boys. A typical spiral. Then she got pregnant at fourteen with her first child, so her dad threw her out their house and she ended up homeless. She was so young and had no one around to really guide her into sensible decisions. And I just thought when I read it that it could have been any of us.'

Adrian, Michael and Charlie all nodded sadly at this. How easily it could have been for any of them to find themselves in the same position as Keira, without the guidance and love they'd received as young people.

'And it made me think,' Becka continued, 'about how much I really wanted to maintain some links with the birth family for the boys. Keira's death prompted me to do a lot of thinking about what I wanted for them growing up, and I want them to really know where they came from. And so...'

At this, Becka clutched Charlie's hand and smiled. And Charlie happily picked up the story. This must be the 'big news' Becka had texted them about the day before, Adrian thought. She'd refused to tell them any more details until today's meet-up and Adrian wondered if it was something to do with the adoption order, knowing the women had submitted their application recently.

'So, we did a thing,' said Charlie. 'We got in touch with Patricia, the twins' social worker, and asked her to help us get in touch with the couple who adopted the twins' sister. She was happy to do it, and so we ended up ringing them last night.'

'I was so nervous!' Becka interjected.

'They're so lovely though, aren't they?' said Charlie. 'And, anyway, we're meeting up next week so the twins can meet their sister. And even better, they only live twenty minutes away, so we can do it regularly from now on if it goes well. How great is that?! She's five years old now and has been with them for nearly two years. She's called Bonnie, and we can't wait to meet her!'

This was great news. Adrian and Michael were overjoyed for their friends. This was adoption, they thought, in all its complexity. Connecting with the birth family, learning about their history, and understanding the children's loss was often heart-breaking and hard. But extending your family, meeting birth siblings and making connections with other adopters through them was a beautiful thing.

Adrian understood Becka's excitement and hoped it went well for them. They knew he'd do the same for Joey one day if it came to it.

Alice

NOW

Earlier, Tegan's heart-rending screams had pierced the air and left Alice and George both on edge. Hair-trigger stress rumbled through the house. It burnt the dinner as they jumped to attention, their child's distress calling the shots as it must. A plate was broken, the dining room a mess of uneaten food and tears. Hours spent on bedtime as the parents worked to calm and quiet, like they did every night.

Kicked, pushed and rejected, Alice sat on the stairs, barely daring to move, until Tegan's breathing calmed and sleep took over. Only then did the tired mum tiptoe down the stairs, avoiding the creaky floorboards with aplomb, hoping for an easier night tonight. Holding her breath.

And now, it was quiet, calm and late, but they refilled their glasses and ignored their watches. The garden, with its murmur of night-time noises, felt safe. Neither Alice nor George wanted to go back into the house. The site of so much of their recent pain. Out here, they could somehow pretend that none of it was happening, it was just the two of them. Together. Enjoying a drink, unwinding from a long day. Sharing stories. Falling asleep on each other's shoulders. Like they'd always done before.

Alice and George had been talking for hours, and now their eyelids were beginning to droop. Tired voices softening with sleep. All evening, heavy words had dropped painfully from their reluctant mouths. And now they sat, staring sadly at the marks those weighted words had left, knowing what they meant. Marks they knew they'd never be able to erase, no matter how much they tried.

Alice shivered from the cool night air. Or perhaps it was from the anxiety thrumming in her chest, she didn't know. She pulled the soft tartan blanket more tightly around her knees and took a sip of the rich, aromatic red wine swirling in the bottom of her glass. It warmed her from the inside. She took a deep breath and savoured the feeling.

Night was falling around her and George as they sat, feet up and sleepy, on the cushioned garden furniture they'd spent a fortune on the year before. They'd thought it would be an investment for them to be comfortable as they sat and watched their child play in the garden they'd worked so hard to make nice. Now they looked at each other sadly, candlelight flickering between them, knowing that once this decision was made, there was no going back.

'I just want her to be happy. I know it sounds simple, and it's not simple. But that's what I want for her, genuinely. But I also think that for her to be happy, something needs to change. And I just don't think it's going to work, keeping her here. She really isn't settled at all, is she?'

Alice's feet were up on George's knee, and she felt, briefly, somewhat better for their chats. She knew that they could face anything together as long as they stayed strong.

'And I just want you to be happy, love.' George replied. 'Yes, I love being a dad. Or at least I would love being a dad if I thought she'd let me be her dad, and if she would accept me. I wanted to be a dad. But you are the most important person in the world to me, Alice. And if you think this isn't going to work, then we need to make that call.'

'And I love you so much for that.' Alice held on tight to her husband's warm hand. 'I love you for saying that. It's not so much that it's difficult, I think I could cope with that, it's more the fact that it feels almost wrong if that makes sense. It feels as though we're keeping her here against her will, and she's just waiting to escape. To escape us and return to her real family, to her real mummy.' Alice sighed and took a sip of wine.

'I want to be her mummy so much. But forcing her to stay with us feels like trying to make a square peg fit in a round hole. We're just not what she wants. We have a little girl who desperately wants to see her birth mother again and a birth mother who desperately wants to see her little girl. And we're the only ones standing between them. I just can't do that. I can't in all good conscience force her to accept us as her new family when she's got a mummy who is there waiting for her. We could try and make this work – make her accept us, kicking and screaming – but how is that good for any of us? I just don't know how I could ever explain that to her in future, that we kept them apart.'

George took a deep breath, stretching his neck and frowning. He knew now that Alice was utterly right. This was so much more complicated than Tegan failing to settle or Alice suffering from post-adoption depression or 'baby blues'. Alice was right in what she said. It ran so much more deeply than that. There had been a fundamental failing in the matching when it came to them and Tegan. Tegan needed to have contact with her birth family, and their presence in her life was keeping her from doing that. Tegan was suffering and as a result, so were they.

They had had a testing week. Tegan was now on holiday from school and struggling. The whole family was feeling the stress of her being at home, with no support, as the girl's rages, frustration and dysregulation ramped up more and more each day. Being at home full-time with no friends, routine, or structure seemed to have triggered Tegan's trauma, and she was displaying more worrying behaviours daily.

'We need to think seriously about what Sami said,' George suggested gently. 'In a way, it might be the best solution for everyone. And perhaps it's come right at the time when we all need it the most, as painful as it seems.'

Sami had visited the family the day before. Relations were strained between her, Alice and George following the letter that had recently fallen on to their doorstep. Still, Alice did her best to appear welcoming.

Showing Sami to the dining room, she brought through three steaming cups of coffee, looking forward to a sit-down, a hot drink and a biscuit while Tegan was settled in front of a Disney film. *Brave*, thought Alice, nostalgically. It had been the first film she and Tegan had watched together after the little girl had come home, she'd seen so much of her feisty new daughter in the lead character with her fiery red hair and her fearless attitude to life. Now, looking at the little girl squashed into the corner of the sofa cuddling an army of soft toys, twirling a strand of that long, curly hair between her fingers, Alice was struck by how tiny and young she looked, how vulnerable.

Lost in her thoughts, Alice was so unprepared for what Sami was to say that after spooning sugar into her coffee, she'd had to ask her to repeat it.

'Okay, so what I was saying was that Piper, Tegan's birth mother, wants to appeal to revoke the placement order for Tegan. She has a solicitor and has lodged her application to appeal with the courts. This isn't something that we would usually worry about when a child is settled in an adoptive placement with a new family. But, well, given the conversations we've had recently, I felt it was something I had to discuss with you. Quite seriously.'

Sami took a moment to look over her notes. She looked at Alice, her expression unreadable. Alice bit down on her lip as all the anxiety of the last few months swirled and rushed through her blood.

'So, as you know, Piper has recently had a baby and moved into a new flat. She has quite significantly turned her life around. Her situation is very different than it was when Tegan was removed from her care. She's worked with social services and accepts where things went so badly wrong, and is ready to do anything to put things right. This is not to say, by any stretch, that it'd be appropriate to have Tegan returned to her, but this is something that we need to be prepared for.'

And it was at that moment that Alice knew that she was no longer going to fight. She could no longer fight to keep a child for whom adoption just wasn't the right choice. She looked at George, and a certain knowledge passed between them at that moment. And Alice knew, almost without doubt, what their decision would be. Fate had intervened, and the decision had been made for them, and nothing they could do would change it now.

Sami

NOW

Sitting at the bar alone, drinking a cold beer, Sami ran her hand through her hair and dialled someone she hadn't spoken to for a long time – Mary. It was the evening after the meeting with Alice and George, and it had been an emotional day.

Mary was in her eighties now, and she and Sami rarely spoke, but no matter how long they left it, Mary was Sami's safe space. Hearing her kind voice calmed Sami straightaway, encouraging her to open up about her day.

Sami had left Alice and George's house earlier, discouraged and angry. One thing she hadn't expected was that they would give up so easily, Sami thought, crossly. Telling Alice and George about Piper's desire to get Tegan back with her wasn't meant to encourage them to give her up.

They were meant to fight for her, to show her how much they want her. Not give her up just like that, Sami fumed as she'd slammed the car door behind her.

They were her parents now. It was their job to protect and fight for Tegan no matter what. Struggling to regulate her emotions, Sami, having given up smoking the year before, reached for the emergency cigarettes in the glove box and lit one, dragging deeply, then coughing sharply.

Driving back to the office through the driving rain, Sami's internal monologue only became angrier. All the careful plans she'd put in place to keep Tegan, Piper, and the new baby happy and settled in their new homes were falling apart around her, and this was unsettling. Stressed, she'd spent the week fielding telephone calls from Piper and Alice to the point where she could no longer answer for fear of losing her temper.

In Sami's job, adoption disruption was something to be avoided at all costs. Preservation of the new family was the goal, with adoption support workers drafted in, when needed, with therapeutic parenting advice to support this aim.

When it became clear that the letter she sent had not had the intended effect, to encourage the adoptive parents to work harder at parenting Tegan and access the support services available, Sami lost patience with Alice and George. The disappointment she felt for what they were doing bubbled underneath now, affecting everything she did and said, shocking Sami with its force.

In the car park at work, Sami had slammed her fists on the dashboard in frustration. Piper was meant to settle with Felix, and Tegan with Alice and George. Both children getting the one-to-one care they needed, pulling them out of their traumatic starts, and giving them the best chance in life. It was how it should be, and now it was going wrong. All because Alice refused to learn to parent this child who needed her so much.

Now, with Mary's kind voice encouraging her to share, Sami began to speak.

'I don't know what to do for the best, Mary. This match was so right, and they are letting her down. I'm so angry with them, I can't think straight.'

Mary allowed Sami to speak, her patient silence allowing Sami to express all the anger and frustration she'd been holding in at work. As always, Mary quickly got to the crux of the matter.

'Sami, dear. I think this girl reminds you of you. And that is entirely normal, my love. She sounds very much like you when they first brought you to me. I know you're angry. But you had contact with your birth mother when you lived with me, and she let you down. Not just once, but many times.

'Just remember, Sami, Tegan is not you, and Piper is not your birth mother. I'm always on your side, and I trust your judgement, but is it possible that this time your personal feelings are clouding your professionalism? Is it possible that, maybe, Tegan would be better off seeing her mum?

'Is it possible that Alice and George are right?'

Adrian

NOW

Adrian couldn't tell you the exact moment he fell in love with his son. But once he did, everything changed. And that, for a man who'd avoided emotional connection for most of his life, was terrifying.

If he were honest, Adrian would tell you that it didn't happen straight away. He wanted to protect Joey, and to be a good dad. He felt a kind of awe for the way the boy put trust in them from the start. But it wasn't love. If he'd tried to sum it up, he'd say that the overriding feeling of the early days was exhaustion, with the day-to-day tasks of caring for Joey being relentless, unrewarding, and met so often with tantrums and fists to his new dads' faces.

As a new adopter, Adrian also felt swamped with expectation. The expectation of being the best parent he could to this child who had lost everything, to heal his trauma, to parent him therapeutically every day, to be the hero his son needed. With all of this running through his head, he admitted that parenting often felt like an exhausting checklist of requirements rather than the labour of love he expected. It was only later, when he read adopter accounts online, that he realised this was completely normal, this feeling of being a babysitter, and began to relax, hoping the love would come later.

But in a way, it was easier then. Emotionally, there was no heart-wrenching tug between them. Adrian felt he'd be okay if it all ended, if Joey, for any reason, no longer lived with them. He'd survive. Yes, he cared for him, and yes, they had some fun times, but on the whole, it was relentlessly difficult. So, if the courts decided Joey would be better off returning to his birth family, Adrian told himself he could live with that.

'Are you ready?' Juliette, the kindly adoption manager with the colourful clothes and braided hair, asks him now as she dashes past, setting up the training room. Adrian, nodding 'yes' and clearing his dry throat, is standing once again in an over-heated hall in a local authority building, waiting for an adoption prep training session to start. Although dressed casually in a soft cashmere jumper and jeans, he could be back at work, ready to give the most important presentation of his life, heavy with the responsibility that what he's about to say might change people's lives. He looks at the nervous couples milling around, sipping coffees impatiently, and remembers the mix of excitement and fear they are experiencing. He smiles as he sees tentative friendships beginning between participants as they mill around the information table, laughing and excitedly sharing their stories.

While he waits, Adrian looks around at the participants in front of him – couples (some straight, some gay), single people, older people, surprisingly young people – and realises, with fondness, how far he and Michael have come. This time, Adrian is on the different side of the table. He is proud to be here as a guest speaker, to speak about his experience of play therapy and how it changed his relationship with Joey.

Adrian remembers the day he and Michael walked into this very room, holding hands, knowing their lives were about to change. He could never at that moment have predicted the emotional rollercoaster they would ride from then on. And it all began in these inauspicious surroundings: the paper sign taped to the door *'Adoption prep training here'*, the terrible coffee, the information table piled high with leaflets, the prospective parents filled with hope, expectation, and so much love to give.

Now chairs were shuffled into lines, throats were cleared, and last-minute coffees were grabbed as the organisers requested that everyone take a seat for the training to begin. Before he knew it, Adrian was standing in front of a small crowd of hopeful faces, being introduced in intimidatingly glowing terms.

'And here we have Adrian,' Juliette smiles over at him. 'He and his husband Michael adopted their son ten months ago and are just about to submit the adoption order paperwork this month!' At this, she pauses as the audience emits a slight hum of admiration, almost a cheer.

'Adrian would be the first to admit that he and Michael did not find things easy with Joey in the beginning. Like many looked-after children, Joey arrived with trauma, having been removed from his birth family and then from his foster family. This is a common experience for adopted children as some will have experienced two or more moves before finding their forever home. As you know, all moves constitute trauma for children, so adopters must be prepared for their children to express grief, loss, anger and anxiety in those early days.

Our adoption support workers can offer an evidence-based programme of play therapy to help new families and their children bond and start to heal their trauma. Adrian and Michael took up this offer and began to see immediate improvements in their relationship with their son. Without saying any more, I'll hand you over to Adrian, who can tell you more about it!'

And with that, Adrian felt as though he were again in his element. Calling on his professional experience, he stepped easily up to the front, confident in addressing these people whose journey he had already walked. He knew how they felt, he knew their anxieties, their concerns, he knew what they wanted to hear. Adrian knew what his message would be.

'Thank you, Juliette!' he smiles at her and then addresses the crowd in front of him.

'Okay, hello everyone, and welcome to prep training. It's an honour to be here today talking about my experience, and I hope that what I'm about to say will help you on your journeys. If not, well, I abdicate all responsibility to

Juliette!' He winks at Juliette, pauses for laughs, then begins as a hush falls across the room.

'So, I will get on to talking about play therapy soon, but I'd like to start with a moment from the last week. The moment I knew I'd fallen in love with my son.

'Every other night, I give my son a bath. I wash his hair, make shampoo quiffs to make him laugh and make glug glug glug noises as we pretend to sink his toy boats in the water. My son was given a hooded towel by his foster carers that we put on the radiator during bath time, ready to wrap him up warm in when he gets out. He loves being wrapped up tight in it as we cuddle him on our knees and one day, I just couldn't get over how unbearably cute he looked in it!

'Usually, I towel-dry his hair as it's so short, it dries quickly. But, on this particular day, he wanted me to use the hairdryer. We ended up playing a game where I would pretend to blow him over using the hairdryer, and he'd do the same to me as I dramatically fell to the floor. In the end, we collapsed giggling on the floor next to each other, and I leant over my son to tickle him.

'Much of the time, I'm going through the motions of the day without looking at him closely. I'm taking care of his needs, feeding, dressing and washing him, making sure he's safe, so I'm not really looking at him like I did at that moment.

'But then, our faces were close, and he looked up at me, holding eye contact and giggled, putting his soft, little hands on either side of my face. I looked deeply into his gorgeous brown eyes, his beautiful baby chubby-cheeked face, and leant over to rub his tiny nose with mine, for an eskimo kiss.

'And at that moment, I felt it. An indescribable feeling of connection as our eyes met, and I knew then that it was love. It was like a rush of emotion for this boy who was suddenly the most beautiful, most incredible, most precious thing to me, and I almost couldn't bear the feeling. But it was love for my boy.

'I realised at that moment, after all of the kicking, fighting and screaming, that the fear had gone, and not only had this little boy had let me into his world, but I had let him into mine. And that was probably one of the most moving moments of my life –apart from my wedding day to my husband, of course!' He held up his hands, feigning a guilty expression.

'And now, I can't unfeel it,' he laughed, as the audience laughed with him. 'I can't stop cuddling him, kissing his head, grabbing him for a squeeze whenever I can until he shouts at me, "Daddddeeeee!" and wriggles to get away. We hug on the sofa watching TV, and I hold on to him tightly, sniffing the top of his beautiful head. I just can't get enough of him. I love him, and I'm his dad. And I never thought we'd get here just a few months ago, when it was all so hard.'

Looking at the faces before him, many now damp with tears, Adrian feels a swell of emotion, suddenly missing his boy with the fiercest of pangs. He sees wives grabbing onto their husbands' hands and squeezing them tight and imagines the loss and pain of infertility that could have brought them to this moment. Single adopters clutch the information packs in their hands, full of hope and trepidation as they embark bravely on this family-building journey without a partner to lean on. Adrian feels a rush of admiration for all of them, and in a way, a nostalgia for the memories he and Michael made here, in this room, with their new friends. He remembers with a smile that first play date he had with Becka and the twins, and the way they'd joked about never speaking at an adoption event. He remembers how hard those early days were, and how much of a relief it was when they passed, unscathed.

'So, now play therapy, and what that meant for us...!' He smiles, continuing his talk, knowing he's engaged the hearts and minds of his audience with the happy ever after ending to his adoption story.

But what Adrian doesn't tell them, or Sami as she guided them through the process of submitting their adoption order application the week before, was that now everything had changed. Love had changed him, and it terrified him like nothing ever had before. Suddenly, his heart was walking around outside of his body, and Adrian felt a vulnerability he'd never experienced, and it hit him hard.

Whenever Adrian had felt this intensity of emotion in the past, he ran. Michael was the only one who'd worked hard enough to chase after him and stop him from running, and their relationship worked well. They were truly in love.

But the intensity of need from a child was something else entirely, and there were days when Adrian shrank from it, fearing the emotion that threatened to overwhelm him. Soon, though, he realised, you can't run from a child who trustingly reaches out their hand to take yours and looks up at you, eyes wide, and calls you 'Daddy', grabbing your heart in both hands as he does.

Applying for the adoption order compounded Adrian's fears in a way he'd never expected. Before he fell in love with his son, the adoption order didn't matter. Whether they applied for it or not seemed an unimportant point of administration at first. But now, putting it in felt enormous, and Adrian needed nothing more than to hear that he was legally Joey's father. And the risk of it being turned down, with either the birth parents contesting it or that the court saying no and returning Joey to his birth mother, was absolutely terrifying. The threats to their little family suddenly felt very real, stealing Adrian's sleep and haunting his thoughts.

This son, this responsibility of his, this beautiful, beautiful boy. One day, he'd have to let him out of his sight, and now, he didn't know if he could bear it.

Peggy

NOW

'Peggy! Peggy? It is you, isn't it?'

The voice behind her was insistent, slightly querulous. Ignoring the impatient young man who nearly walked into her, tutting, Peggy stopped, tucked the newspaper she'd just bought under her arm and rearranged the heavy shopping bags digging into her hands. The day had turned hot and sunny, and she was looking forward to getting home and sitting down with a nice cup of tea. After shopping for groceries and cleaning the house, Peggy had a busy evening ahead of her, driving both of her foster boys to contact with their birth parents after school. Before then, she had hoped for a quiet hour to sit down with a Battenburg cake and her favourite quiz shows.

'Peggy, it's Piper. It's been a while.'

Peggy smiled at the girl, taking in her improved appearance. With the baby tucked into a sling and nuzzling contentedly against her chest, Piper looked happy, clean and presentable, although slightly wan and tired around the eyes with her hair pulled into a messy, low ponytail. Par for the course for a new mum, thought Peggy. She cooed over the soft head of the beautiful new baby boy, now grizzling a little as the gentle rocking of Piper's step had stopped. But then Peggy remembered, with some sadness, the last time she'd seen Piper.

The two women knew each other from meeting during family contacts between Piper and Tegan while the child had been in foster care. These contact sessions had taken place twice or three times a week at first but had diminished in regularity in the period before Tegan was placed with Alice and George, as is the usual protocol.

The last family contact had been distressing for everyone involved. As an experienced foster carer, Peggy had seen it all play out before, but it never stopped being heart-breaking to watch. A distraught Piper had upset Tegan with her visible misery, grabbing her arm as she left, crying, shouting and begging the contact facilitators not to take her child. As Tegan had been led, sobbing, from the room, Piper had yelled after her, 'I'll get you back. I'll get you back with me. Things have changed, you'll see!'

Peggy empathised with the woman's heartbreak, there could be nothing more painful than seeing your child being taken away to be adopted, knowing there's a chance you'll never see them again. But she also couldn't condone the way that Piper behaved, knowing how much confusion it had bred in Tegan's young mind and the conflicting messages it had given her immediately before moving to her new family. The little girl was old enough to know and love her mother but not quite mature enough to understand the complexities of adoption. The poor mite had so little chance of settling well given such a difficult start, thought Peggy.

Now, though, Peggy was happy to see that the young woman in front of her was clearly doing an excellent job with her new baby and was relieved that she was up and about, dressed, and seeming to be on top of things. Peggy knew that that was half the battle with a new-born.

'How are you, pet? Lovely to see you and the little one. How's everything been? I hope you're managing okay, duck.'

Ignoring niceties, Piper looked directly at Peggy, her voice emphatic when she asked, 'How's Tegan, Peggy? Have you seen her? They won't tell me anything, and I just need to know how she's getting on. I'm worried sick for my little girl, Peggy. Tell me anything, I just need to know she's okay.'

As people milled in and out of the shops around them, flowing around the two women like a river around two immovable stones, Peggy knew that at that moment, time stood still. Nothing else mattered to Piper apart from her children. Oblivious to the world around her, the focus was on getting her children back with her. She knew she would not able to rest until she could kiss both of their heads, hold their hands and be sure that they were safe. Piper would fight until she was a mother of two again. Peggy didn't always see that fight in the eyes of the birth parents she met, but when she did, she recognised it for what it was. A parent who has seen rock bottom, lost the people most precious to her, and realised too late just what it is that she's lost.

Thinking of the worried texts she'd recently received from Alice and the long telephone call she'd had with Sami the night before, Peggy knew that she could quickly allay Piper's fears and offer her some hope of seeing Tegan again. However, she knew that nothing had been decided yet, and that, even if it was, it wasn't her place to tell Piper anything just yet. She'd get in trouble if she did. Her heart swelled with the enormity of the emotions surrounding this case. She'd known that adoption wasn't right for this child, she wished she'd been listened to. But somehow, it felt as though things were coming right again, as sad as that was for Alice and George, she thought.

'You know I can't tell you anything, my love. But I know that the new parents are good people, and I can tell you that they will do right by Tegan. Trust me, dear.

'Now you go and enjoy that gorgeous boy of yours. Everything else will come right. Go be a mum and give him some extra snuggles from me. Take care, Piper.'

And as Piper turned to walk away, Peggy noticed the way the younger woman's arm tightened reflexively around the precious bundle strapped to her chest, and somehow, Peggy knew that Piper would get it right this time. She didn't know how she knew, but she did.

Piper had made mistakes, she'd hit rock bottom, but now the young woman had found her strength, her motherhood. It may have been too late to keep Tegan with her the first time, but she'd found it now. And Peggy crossed her fingers behind her back as she prayed a silent prayer that Piper never let it go.

Suddenly, thinking of something she needed to ask, Peggy called after Piper before she disappeared into the crowd.

'Piper, love. I didn't ask you the baby's name. What did you call him? Gorgeous wee chap he is!'

Piper turned and smiled, looking lovingly down at her baby's soft, warm head.

'His name's Felix,' she said quietly. 'It means happiness.'

Alice

NOW

'What if it's all because of me?' asked Alice.

It was 1:00 p.m., and Tegan was at holiday club. Alice and George had decided it was best for her, and Sami agreed. Spending so much time at home seemed to trigger Tegan's memories of the past – the cold, hungry days she'd spent at home with Piper – so they all agreed that some normality and routine would do her good before the big move the following week. The little girl had skipped into school happily, excited to see her friends, even though there were only five other children there.

With Tegan out of the house, George took a day off work so he and Alice had a day together. They decided to make the most of it by walking along the river with the dog.

'What do you mean, love?' asked George now, looking out over the water.

'I thought I was healed.' Alice replied. 'That I'd done the work from my past, and it couldn't hurt me anymore. It was such a long time ago now, but those scars run deep, and I can't forget the way Axel shouted at and insulted me quite so easily. It was the way he made me feel, you know? There were some days that I prayed for quiet, that he'd leave me alone. And even then, I could hear his insults ringing in my ears.'

George listened patiently as Alice continued.

'Eventually, it got so bad that even when he started to speak to me normally, my heart rate would rise, and my palms would begin to sweat. I was on high alert, expecting him to get angry at any moment. I could never relax, thinking he was about to explode.

'In so many ways, I can see myself in Tegan. She's lived with violence and aggression. And she's a little girl. So vulnerable. She had no power to leave or to get away from what was frightening her. When she came to live with us and cried, screamed or shouted, I could see myself in her. Feeling frightened, cornered, on edge, on a constant lookout for danger.

'But it triggered me too. Some days when Tegan screamed, I would try to be there for her. Try to be the safe space, the calm, therapeutic mum she needed. But other times, I can't deny that it took me right back to how I felt when I was with Axel, and I could feel myself shutting down. Wanting to get away from her, to find some quiet and make the screaming stop.

'And now I can't help thinking I'm a terrible mum because I couldn't overcome that for her. I wish I could have been the mum that she needs.'

George could see the internal torment that Alice was going through. The night before, they had spoken at length about Tegan's transition back to Peggy's home. Alice and George both agreed that it was the best thing for them, Tegan and, they hoped, for Piper. But now, in the light of day, George could see that doubt was creeping in for Alice.

Sitting down on a bench, George took Alice's hand.

'Do you remember what we talked about when Sami first mentioned Piper's request to have Tegan home?' he began gently.

'We agreed that Tegan needs Piper, and Piper needs Tegan. Alice, sweetheart, I know you blame yourself. You were so determined to be the best mum you could be, and you wanted to make life better for Tegan. It's just the kind of person you are, and it's what I love about you. But no matter how good a mum you were, it wouldn't have changed that fact.

'Tegan came into our lives, and we tried to give her all of the love we had. She had experienced trauma, and we wanted to help her. But all of the love we gave was never going to fix the fact that she knew her birth mum was out there and ready to bring her home. That's not our fault, and it's not hers either. It's just the way it is.

'Some things are just not meant to be, and although it's not what we wanted, maybe what we're doing now is what we were always meant to do. It was our job to find Tegan and advocate for what's best for her, and that's what we're doing.

'I know it's been unbelievably hard, and I know the trauma of it has triggered some incredible pain for you, Alice. But please, believe me when I say it's not your fault. I know the triggers of the past make you feel weak, but as far as I'm concerned, you're the strongest woman in the world. You're fighting for what's best for Tegan, despite the loss it means for us. To me, that is strength, and I love you all the more for it.'

As they stand by the river, they gaze into the water at their reflections. Two people, side by side, holding hands and standing firm. A bubbly puppy bounding up to greet them, making them both smile despite the gravity of the day. Seeing herself reflected in the water, Alice is so grateful for this man by her side.

And as they turn back for home, together, Alice can't help but think of the similarities between herself and Piper. They were both young when they found themselves involved with dangerous, abusive men. They were both suffering the loss of their child, or the chance to have a child as a result. They are both strong women, Alice thinks, who have fought hard to get themselves back on their feet.

Feeling a pang of female solidarity with Piper, a woman she's never met, Alice takes strength from their shared experience, reflecting on the love they both feel for this child who has touched their lives. And the shared drive they both have to see this child thrive. Everything they do is for their daughter, Tegan.

Charlie

NOW

Charlie got up from the park bench where she'd been reading a book, or at least meaning to, to greet Alice with a wave. The sun was out, and realising she'd read the same line over a few times now, Charlie had let her eyes close for a moment, enjoying its warmth. Woken in time by her Fitbit telling her it was time to move, she spotted Alice heading towards her. Charlie sat up, yawned and smiled. It certainly was tiring being a parent to twins.

Charlie had taken advantage of the lovely weather to walk around the lake, feeding the ducks on the way with the crusts of a sandwich she'd finished earlier. She felt refreshed for having the break but reflected on how strange and oddly freeing it felt, being in a park without her wife and the twins after spending so much time together lately. Indeed, she jumped in alarm a few times while walking, thinking she heard the phantom cries of her children before remembering they were safe at home with their other mum.

Alice had texted the night before asking to meet, and Charlie, surprised but pleased that she'd reached out, had arranged to walk and talk in the park today. Remembering the abrupt conversation they'd had following the party at Adrian and Michael's house, Charlie hoped that Alice would now be able to confide in her more openly about some of her difficulties with Tegan.

'Tread gently,' Becka had advised, jiggling one of the twins on her hip, after planting a kiss on her wife's cheek as she got ready to leave the house. 'She's feeling so vulnerable right now. I can't imagine what they're going through.'

Knowing this, Charlie wasn't sure why Alice had asked her to meet. She was aware that she wasn't the most approachable out of her and her wife. Becka was the softer

217

of the two, being sweet, caring and maternal to everyone she met. Whereas Charlie was more outspoken, and much more likely to call a spade a spade. But maybe that was what Alice needed right now, she thought. That and the fact that Charlie had experience as a social worker. Heeding her wife's warning, though, she resolved to approach whatever Alice told her with a considered gentleness and restraint.

She had reflected on what Alice had told them both lately over text messages, as well as the brief conversations they'd had at Adrian and Michael's party. Charlie wondered what caused her to look so down, and her professional training led her to look for clues. She'd seen the drawn look on Alice's face and the sadness evident in her demeanour. Those, combined with the distracted, stressed way she interacted with Tegan, all told a story that Alice's words were not saying.

When talking to Becka about ways they could help, Charlie had remembered a case that she'd dealt with during her social worker days. A young adoptive mother had come into the social services offices, demanding to see her. Her face had been streaked with tears, but her eyes were hard and determined. The woman had almost yelled at Charlie, saying that a social worker had better be there to collect her daughter from school that evening because she couldn't do it herself. She'd had enough, and she was walking away.

On closer examination, and a gentle conversation over a hot cup of tea, it had become clear that the woman was suffering from compassion fatigue. Caring for an adopted child with attachment disorder could be challenging. The last straw had been an extreme meltdown suffered by this child while her mum was driving her to school. The child had screamed, kicked the back of the seat, banged on the glass window and pulled off her seatbelt, finally climbing over the seats to shout at her mum in the driving seat. The mum, exhausted from lack of sleep, had panicked, scared that the stress of driving under those conditions would make her crash while driving. So she stopped the car, and melted into tears. Managing, shakily, to call a friend to take her daughter to school, the mum had driven straight to the social services offices, crying, desperate for help.

Charlie's training had taught her that the symptoms of compassion fatigue were often hard to spot. Still, the exhaustion, the feeling of having 'had enough', a lack of connection with your child, and a desperate need for help or a break were common signs. As an older adopted child, Tegan could be displaying signs of trauma that would disrupt attachment and family life, meaning that Alice was more than likely suffering from compassion fatigue, with a dose of depression mixed in. It was all too common in adoption and often hard to solve. These children often needed so much more care than adoptive families were able or qualified to provide alone.

Charlie, sadly, wished she could do more to get Alice to see that all they wanted to do was support her. There was no shame in finding it all incredibly hard. She prepared herself to gently broach the topic of compassion fatigue and support services with her friend. However, she found herself unprepared for the conversation she was about to have.

'Hi, Charlie!' Alice smiled, and the first thing Charlie noticed was that Alice looked lighter. There was something about her that looked, not positive as such, but as if a heavy weight had been lifted from her shoulders. There was life in her eyes again, an energy that was missing when they saw each other last. Her gait was purposeful, and her greeting strong. Charlie wondered what had changed.

Sitting down on the bench together, they watched as a family of ducklings swam away confidently from their mother as she paddled lazily behind them. The water rippled gently in their wake, and sunrays dappled on its surface.

Alice, clearing her throat, looked at Charlie and began to speak.

'It's not the way we wanted our story with Tegan to end, and I could never have imagined that my journey to be a mum would end this way. But it feels as though we've found a way to put her story back on the right path again. And somehow, that feels like the only thing we can do. I know because I wake up feeling calm these days, not filled with stress like I have been for months. I used to feel as though I was somehow doing something really wrong. Nothing felt right, and the pieces didn't fit. But now they do, even though we never wanted this to happen, and could never have planned it this way.

'Tomorrow, we begin virtual re-introductions for Peggy and Tegan. And Peggy will take over and do what we can't, which is allow Tegan to work on herself without the pressure of attaching to new parents for a while. And when she's ready, she will find her own birth mother again, and they'll have each other. They'll get through it all together, as a family. I don't know why, and I couldn't tell you exactly how I know, but something tells me this is what we needed to do.'

As Charlie patiently listened, she came to understand precisely how Alice felt, and she felt growing awe of the strength of her friend. And perhaps because she knew what a fantastic parent Alice could be, when given the chance, the question leapt out of her mouth before she could stop herself.

'Do you think you'll adopt again?' she asked instinctively. 'Oh, Alice, I'm sorry, is that an insensitive question?'

'No, it's okay,' Alice replied, looking thoughtful. 'Of course, it's something George and I have talked about, over and over again. But it's such a difficult one to answer. Right now, everything is too raw, and Tegan hasn't even moved back to Peggy's house yet, so we're just in a kind of limbo state.

'We did so much preparation for Tegan's arrival. So much wishing, waiting and hoping, as well as preparing our hearts, minds and our home. She grew in my heart, and it will take time to get over her, time for my heart and mind to catch up with the fact that I'm no longer a mother. I know I need to grieve. I owe it to her and to myself to grieve and not move on too quickly.

'Emotionally, I invested everything in being her mum, and all of this has taken so much from me. I feel exhausted and drained. And it's not just the last year that has been difficult. It came after years of trying for a baby, years of infertility, IVF, pregnancy, and loss. I don't know if I can take any more heartache. Physically, emotionally, mentally, I just feel spent, you know?'

Charlie couldn't imagine exactly how her friend felt, but as she listened to Alice's words, she could feel the immensity of what she had lost. If she had been through the same, she didn't know whether she would be able to find the strength to carry on with the demanding journey of becoming a parent.

'And,' Alice continued, 'we don't even know if we'd be allowed to adopt again, either. We know that we made the very best decision for Tegan, and for all of us, to enable her and Piper to move on with their lives. But in the eyes of adoption agencies, we disrupted an adoption. And to many of them, it's as simple as that. I've read stories of families blacklisted as adopters after a disruption, without being given a chance to try again.

'And even if we could fight it, persuading them that we're good parents again after all of this, well, even the thought of it exhausts me right now. The process of IVF demands everything from you physically, but with adoption it's also mentally. Having spent the last few years doing both, I think I need a complete break. I need to remember who I am again. To enjoy my life again. I owe it to myself, and to George.'

Charlie, wanting to reply angrily to the comment around 'blacklisting', bit her tongue, knowing that her righteous indignation was the last thing her friend needed right now. She'd save it for her debrief with Becka later. But inside, she was fuming because she knew that Alice was right, this would jeopardise their chance to adopt again. And yet, any adoption agency would be lucky to have Alice and George on their books as adopters. They're the bravest, strongest people she knows.

Charlie knew that her friend had waited so long to be a mum. She had been through every possible trial to get there, and now, she was giving up that chance because she knew it was in the child's very best interests.

As the two women got up to leave the park, walking side by side, Charlie knew her friend's actions were driven by selflessness. A desire to do the very best she could for a child, even if it meant losing her chance to be a mother. She was putting the needs of the child before her own.

And perhaps, Charlie thought, is that not the ultimate test of strength in motherhood, in the end?

Becka and Adrian

NOW

It was a 'proud parent' day for two of the couples as Adrian and Michael were taking Joey to visit the contact centre where they'd volunteered in preparation to become his parents, and Becka and Charlie were taking Parker and Phoenix to meet their sister. They were all very excited.

Charlie, in pyjamas, was making bacon sandwiches that morning as the boys, dressed in nothing but their nappies, were shouting happily at each other as they played, upending the toy box with a crash. Becka grabbed a coffee and popped in and out of the kitchen with different outfits for the boys, struggling to choose. A shopping trip the day before had seen her return home, arms heavy with bags full of cute outfits that she squashed into the boys' bedroom drawers before Charlie could question them.

'Sit down for a minute!' Charlie laughed. 'Come on, eat something! We don't have to leave for another hour or so, and the boys don't care what they wear. Have a bacon sarnie and a cuppa, and try to relax, love!'

Becka laughed at herself. It was crazy how nervous and excited she felt. Although she knew she was getting ahead of herself, she wouldn't have mentioned this to anyone just yet, but it felt as though she were gaining an extra child. And a daughter at that!

Becka loved her boys with a passion and had never cared what gender her children were, but the idea of gaining an almost-daughter filled her with joy. She paused for a moment at the thought, remembering Alice's impending loss of her almost-daughter and felt a bittersweet mix of emotions at how differently their stories had turned out.

Well, she thought, we'll just have to share, won't we? We're one big family, and that's that.

'Hi Bonnie, it's Auntie Becka,' she whispered, smiling at her reflection. Becka already had two beautiful nieces, her sister's children, and the days they were born had been two of the most exciting days of her life. She'd never forget the feeling of rushing to the hospital, laden with soft new outfits, flowers and balloons, desperate for those first tender cuddles.

Today felt the same for Becka, a day she'd never forget.

The day before, they'd shown Parker and Phoenix a photo book they'd been sent by Bonnie's parents, full of pictures of the boys' sister and her family. Much like the life story book, Becka and Charlie hoped that the picture book would help prepare them for the idea of having a sister in their lives who didn't live with them, both before and after the visit. Becka pointed at Bonnie and said, 'She's your sister, Bonnie!' and both boys repeated 'sister' after her.

Soon it was time to leave, with the twins looking handsome in the shorts and shirt sets Becka had picked out, accessorised with cute new caps and sunglasses. Loading the boys into the car with a picnic and a bag full of all of the essentials they travelled with now as parents of toddler twins, they set off for the park, excitement and anticipation building in their bellies.

At the same time, Adrian and Michael were taking Joey by the hand, leading him up the stairs to the contact centre. It was the end of the morning session, and they hoped to find Marjorie there, relaxing with a cup of tea after the rush. Joey didn't understand what they were doing but was excited to get inside all the same, pulling on his dads' arms impatiently. Adrian hoped that Marjorie hadn't completely tidied all of the toys away so that Joey could play while they had a chance to catch up.

Breaking free from their arms, Joey ran into the building and was met by a grinning Marjorie, delight written all over her face to meet the son she knew Adrian and Michael had worked so hard for.

'Who's this gorgeous boy then?! You must be Joey. And you're so big! You must be, what, six years old? What a big grown-up boy!'

Joey giggled at the fuss, indignantly informing her that he was only three, and was happy to be led off by Marjorie to find a chocolate biscuit in the kitchen as Adrian and Michael trailed behind.

When they returned, Marjorie hugged both of the men in turn.

'He's a gorgeous little chap. You should be so proud. I know it's not been easy for you both, but he's lovely. You've done such a good job with him, and you can see how happy he is and settled. I'm proud of you both,' she finished, wiping away a tear from her eye. 'And, when I said you were coming in today with your boy, there was someone else who wanted to say hello. She's been waiting for you.'

Adrian turned around to see a familiar figure sitting patiently waiting in the corner. It was Ruby. Now she came over to meet them. She looked better, calmer and more neatly presented than the last time they'd met. Ruby's eyes were kind as she spoke, softly.

'You were always so good and kind to me when I was struggling. You helped my daughter, made sure she always had nice things to play with and helped make her feel safe here at the centre. I'll never forget that.

'When Marjorie told me you were coming in today, I wanted to stay for a while to see you and say thank you. It's a beautiful gift having a child, and from the moment I met you both, I knew you'd make excellent parents. You have that kindness in you to make a difference in a child's life.

'You have a fantastic lad there, I can only imagine how hard you've worked with him to help him feel so safe and loved, and you can see it in his eyes how happy he is,' she said with a smile, seeing Joey now on Michael's shoulders, playing with his dad's hair.

'So, I just wanted to say thank you. I'm doing well, I'm back on my meds and sorting my life out, and my daughter's doing great at school, thanks to my parents. This contact centre helped save our relationship, and you were a massive part of that. Good luck, enjoy your family, and enjoy that boy of yours. I wish you all the best.'

Moved by this speech, Adrian was choked up and could do nothing but pull Ruby into a tight hug. It meant so much to him to hear her words, the words he'd never heard from his mum. Something inside him felt a kind of completeness, contentment now, hearing them from Ruby. It was as if he heard his own mum's voice coming through in Ruby's words. And as they said goodbye, he knew he would take that home with him. The blessing to go ahead and enjoy family life, to let himself love and be loved, and to open himself up to all of the potential fear, vulnerability, and emotional complexity that came with it. Taking Michael's hand, the family said goodbye to Marjorie and Ruby and left the centre, their happy little family more secure and tightly attached than ever.

Across the city, Becka and Charlie were having a similar experience as they watched their little boys toddle nervously towards a small, blonde stranger who had just asked them to play. As soon as they saw Bonnie, they knew she had to be Parker and Phoenix's sister. She had their blonde hair, their curls, their bright blue eyes and the same dotted freckles across her nose. She stood with the twins now with a big smile on her face as though she knew them already. The photobooks that Becka and Charlie had sent over, similar ones to the book they'd received from Bonnie's parents, had done the trick.

Bringing the three children together to meet and play was reuniting a family, and something within Becka and Charlie felt right again after the loss of Keira. It felt as though they were honouring her memory in bringing her children back together.

'This is what Keira would have wanted, I'm sure,' said Becka to her wife, as they greeted Bonnie's parents with a wave.

Joy, Bonnie's mum, was laying out a picnic while her husband, Tom, supervised the children on the play equipment. Becka and Charlie lent a hand, and once everything was ready, they all sat down to eat. Bonnie was already taking charge and seating one twin on either side of her, telling everyone they were her little brothers, and making sure they had plenty of crisps on their plates.

'I think it's been tricky for her,' started Joy. 'It was quite a traumatic time for her when Keira had the twins, as she was left alone and then suddenly removed from everything she knew. She's blocked a lot of it out, but she knew her mum was having a baby. We've talked to her about the twins, but we never knew whether or not she'd get to meet them. The day we got your call was so exciting for all of us, and she's spoken of nothing else since. She knew she had a brother or sister, but having two brothers all at once is like having all her dreams come true!'

And Becka could only agree. Meeting such lovely people who were open to meeting other members of their daughter's family, establishing a friendship with them, and introducing their sons to their biological sister, who would hopefully be there for them for the rest of their lives, was everything she could have hoped for. Forming bonds of family and friendship that would last a lifetime.

It doesn't get much better than this, Becka thought. A dream come true for us all. Our family, everyone included, is complete.

All the pieces of the jigsaw were coming back together, and it felt so good.

Adrian

THEN

Grieving his mother – his complicated, wonderful, infuriating mother – was the hardest thing Adrian had ever had to do. How do you mourn the death of someone you've loved yet missed your whole life?

The texts came in one day, on a bright summer's evening in the city, and Adrian was sitting outside at a bar by the river with a crisp, cold pint in his hand. He ignored them, knowing who they were from, and focused on his friends, knowing they asked nothing more of him than banter and beers.

And that, thought Adrian, is fine with me.

'Call me, please!' went unanswered, unseen. The urgency unfelt by Adrian as he turned the screen away, not wanting to know.

When Adrian finally spoke to his dad later that evening, his voice gave out as he stood alone in his immaculate city apartment, looking out at the dark, starry night. He remembered the little boy he'd been at the parties his mum had held and felt a sadness he'd never felt before. Sadness for the family they'd tried to be, sadness for the childhood loneliness he'd felt. Sorrow for a beautiful, wonderful woman who never got the help she needed, and for the son she worked so hard to please without seeing the love he already had for her.

All I wanted, Adrian thought, was for her to see me, to listen to me.

To know that the school project made of toilet rolls and tissue paper meant more to him than all the extravagant parties in the world, and a simple 'I'm so proud of you!' from his mum would have made his day every time.

But now she was gone, and Adrian didn't know what to do.

'Fuck this,' he muttered, throwing his glass of whisky angrily across the beautifully decorated room, watching numbly as it smashed on the expensive glass coffee table. He slumped to the floor in front of the picture windows looking out over the city, and sobbed as the glass reflected his tears.

He had everything he'd ever dreamed of, and life was so good. Why did this have to happen now? This unwelcome assault on his emotions that he had no idea how to fight.

His phone buzzed again and again. He turned off the ringer, switched it off and threw it across the room after the drink. He didn't need anyone, and certainly not now. But then the door buzzer was ringing, and he couldn't ignore it.

'Not now,' he shouted as he stumbled past the broken glass, the whisky, and the phone he wanted gone, towards the door that signalled yet another intrusion into his perfectly ordered life.

But he couldn't block out the voice of the man he'd already tried to leave. The man he loved but couldn't yet tell. The firm, kind voice that broke through his tears.

Michael's words were to change his life forever from that day.

'I'm here,' he said, loudly and clearly. 'And I'm not leaving just yet. I understand if you can't let me in, but I'm here for you, Adrian. And if you need me, I'll stay. I'll wait as long as it takes, because I love you.'

And just like that, Adrian's heart cracked open with grief and love as he opened the door to see Michael sitting patiently in the hall, with a six-pack of beer in his hands. Knowing that he was still there, despite the missed calls and the fights, was the day their relationship really began, and the work of healing commenced.

Alice

NOW

'Look at her,' Alice whispered, nudging George, who was standing next to her, grabbing a quick sandwich lunch between work calls. He looked up and then over at Tegan, whilst holding Alice's hand.

Tegan was sitting calmly in the living room, smiling, as she chatted to Peggy via video call. Alice's heart filled with tenderness for the little girl who looked so young, and small, curled up in the corner of the big armchair under the window. She had pulled a soft blanket over her knees and tucked several of her teddies in next to her as she chatted animatedly to her former foster carer, twirling her plaits between her fingers. Alice overheard her earnest complaints about missing school during the holidays, hating being at home, and not being able to see her friends every day. From the kitchen, Alice could also hear Peggy's reassuring tones calmly letting Tegan know that she is safe, and she is heard. It both warms and breaks Alice's heart a little to see just how much Tegan relaxes in Peggy's presence, even if it's only virtual.

The night before, Tegan had lashed out angrily when Alice had tried to clean her teeth before bed. Crying, shouting and throwing the brush across the room, she'd eventually collapsed, sobbing, against Alice's shoulder. 'I just want my mummy,' she'd whispered, as Alice had stroked her hair.

'I know, lovely. I know,' she'd murmured, hoping the girl knew just how much she understood.

There had been a shift in the household over the last week. Since their last meeting with Sami, preparations were taking place quietly behind the scenes to transition Tegan back to Peggy's home. The first step in this process was the introduction of regular video calls with Peggy that Tegan loved. The transition would be made more straightforward, for Tegan at least, because she already knew and loved Peggy.

Tegan trusted Peggy to keep her safe, trusted her to look after her, but there was no pressure for her to accept Peggy as her mother. She knew that she wasn't. That was the difference, Alice thought, between foster care and adoption.

When Tegan had lived with Peggy, she knew that she'd have regular contact with her mother. However, when she moved in with Alice and George, she was told that she had to accept them as her new parents and forget her birth mum completely. Tegan had been through a lot and survived so much in her short life, but forgetting her birth mother and replacing her overnight was one expectation too far. Alice didn't blame the little girl for the outbursts of anger she expressed when finding herself in a situation that was simply impossible for her to accept.

Now that the decision had been made to transition Tegan back to Peggy's house, Alice felt that relations between her and the child had become more manageable. The little girl didn't know yet that she'd be moving, but Alice did. The enormous pressure that she'd put on herself to replace a mother who was irreplaceable to Tegan was now gone. She was never going to fill that role, and now she didn't have to worry that she must appear to. Tegan's moods were still volatile, and they saw tantrums and angry outbursts every day, but Alice no longer took these personally, which made them so much easier to deal with.

Although it may have seemed strange to an outsider looking in, Alice felt softer and more understanding towards her daughter now that she had made the difficult decision to let her go. Yes, she was grieving. Alice was mourning her chance to be a mother, but at the same time, she felt an enormous sense of rightness. It was as if everything that had been wrong for such a long time was now becoming right again.

Sami was at pains to remind them that there would be no perfect, rose-tinted reunion. Tegan was removed from Piper's care for very valid and serious reasons, and they needed to be exceptionally careful. The reintroduction of Piper to Tegan would go very slowly and at the child's pace. Tegan may miss her mummy, and Piper may have turned her life around, but a lot had happened and changed in both their lives since they'd last seen each other. A lot of work needs to be done to ensure that the reunification is successful and doesn't cause Tegan further trauma.

Alice knew and understood all of this and, despite their recent differences, trusted Sami to get it right for Tegan. She knew it wasn't going to be an easy ride. But, from what Sami had said, it sounded as though Piper had genuinely turned her life around for the better. Surely, she and Tegan deserved a second chance at a life together. And Peggy would be there for Tegan every step of the way, a woman Alice would trust with her life. She knew that Tegan would be in safe hands with her.

Peggy, Sami, and the adoption support team will also provide therapeutic support for Tegan. They will work to help her feel safe, to address the trauma and attachment difficulties brought on by her early years, and to work through the scars of the neglect she has suffered. With the pressure of accepting new parents and attaching to a new family taken away, she can relax into the therapeutic foster care expertise of Peggy's warm, loving home. Then, when she's ready, she can be introduced, little by little, to her birth mother in the hope that they will both be able to heal and move on together.

Now, Alice is gazing out of her kitchen window, listening contentedly to the sound of Tegan chatting happily to Peggy in the background. The sun is shining brightly, and it is a beautiful day. Despite the ever-present sadness that sits heavily on her heart, Alice's thoughts feel clear and bright for the first time in a long time.

A calm came over Alice when she imagined Tegan seeing her birth mother again. She smiled as she imagined herself handing Tegan over to Piper. Watching them run away from her, Tegan chatting happily to her mum, telling her everything she'd missed.

Here you go. She's yours. I have brought her back to you, she thinks, sadly. She is reminded of Keira and how she tragically hadn't had an opportunity to see any of her three young children again before she died. And of Becka and Charlie, doing such an incredible job raising those beautiful boys who seemed in so many ways just meant to be theirs.

And herself and George. She doesn't know what the future holds for them, but she knows it looks very different from how either of them had imagined. One day at a time, Alice thinks, wiping away a single tear as it rolls soundlessly down her cheek.

****

George had left them the key. He'd taken Alice to her mother's so that she would stay curled up and regressive in her mother's arms for days.

The friends met and entered the house. Reverent with the enormity of the task they'd been given, they fell quiet. The women started in the bedroom where Alice had left Tegan's clothes, freshly laundered on the bed. Putting all emotion to one side, they set to work, folding and packing. Organising the small soft clothes into new suitcases as if getting ready for a family holiday that would never happen.

They packed and tidied all morning. Tegan's toys, clothes, bedding, and belongings would be loaded into the boot of Becka's car to be dropped off at Peggy's house later that day. Mementoes of motherhood – framed family photographs, ornaments and pictures drawn by a five-year-old's hand – were all carefully packed into a memory box chosen especially for the occasion by Charlie. Alice may not be able to look at them now, but one day they would mean the world.

The men worked downstairs. Removing the garden toys and the bike, dismantling the swing set, and clearing the garden of the evidence of childhood. They then began replanting bulbs that would soon bear colourful blooms to replace the colourful plastic as it went. Once this was done, they scanned the downstairs rooms. So much of the brief life of a child was contained there. School newsletters on the pinboard, paintings blue-tacked to the wall, a doll, naked, in the downstairs toilet, its half-shorn head poking out from the bin.

They cleaned and sorted, wiped pen marks from walls and removed fingerprints from paintwork. Adrian hesitated just a moment before erasing a wobbly 'Mummy' written in chalk in the playroom on the wall painted as a blackboard by George just months before.

Underneath it all, there were the scars. When they peeled away the layers – the toys, clothes and paintings – trauma was revealed below. A split in a doorframe, blood smeared on a wall, muddy footprints where the walls had been kicked. Over and over. A bin full of ornaments smashed beyond repair. A blind pulled down from a window. Wallpaper picked at compulsively, and then torn from the wall. Sharp shards of broken plastic hidden deep within the folds of the young girl's bedding. Charlie began to think of Alice's face, lined with worry.

'I checked her room every day. But it just wasn't enough.'

The friends patched it all up, their hearts heavy for the house's three occupants. Now two, once more. Becka, in the kitchen, carefully packed away Alice's treasured 'Mummy' mug in swathes of tissue paper, replacing it with a mug she'd chosen especially for her friend as a surprise. A new inscription for her to find when she returned.

And when the job was done, the group of friends plumped up the cushions and placed fresh, brightly coloured flowers and chocolates on the coffee table, working to imbue this home with as much love as their friendship could provide, warding off sadness in the only way they knew how. Wrapping Alice and George in the gentle nurture they were so practised at giving their children, hoping it will help them heal.

****

Alice and George arrived slightly late to the party, letting themselves in through the side gate, following the sounds of happy voices to the garden at the back of Adrian and Michael's rambling Victorian home. Alice clutched congratulations cards, gift bags and flowers, while George carried two bottles of wine. Soft white fairy lights twinkled on the trellis, colourful balloons and streamers were tied to the gate posts, and the joyous chattering of children and grown-ups filled the air.

'So good to see you both.' Adrian, in shorts, a vest and sandals, greeted them warmly as they entered the garden, accepting their gifts with a smile. 'Michael's just firing up the barbeque, so he'll be around in, well, let's give it a few hours, I'd say! So glad you could come. Joey will be so excited to see you. Make yourselves at home!'

Friends and relatives gathered in small groups in the beautiful garden, which was decorated prettily in the style of a vintage country fair, bunting strung over the doorframes, tealights on tables and a rag rug covered in toys on the deck. The sun was shining, and it was a beautiful day. Jugs of ice-cold homemade lemonade glistened in the heat, and Alice heard a soft pop as a champagne bottle opened to cheers the occasion.

As Alice greeted Adrian, she saw George intercept a ball rolling towards him, kicking it back to Joey who happily engaged in a game of football with him, and who ended up chasing George, giggling, around the lawn.

A sharp pang of sadness clutched at Alice's heart, freezing her in place for a moment as she remembered the last time they'd been here. The game that could have gone so wrong. The moment they witnessed the expression of Tegan's frustration and pain, and the fear it had brought to all of them. The feeling of helplessness it caused.

Now, seeing Joey so healthy, happy and loved as he ran around the garden, surrounded by family, brought Alice a strange sense of contentment mixed with sadness for herself. It wasn't unusual for Alice to become caught in these moments where the emotion of the year overwhelmed her and tugged at her breath. She knew it would take time, and that processing all the changes they'd had would be anything but easy.

Surrounded by her friends on this beautiful midsummer's day, she felt a new wistful emotion as she imagined how things could have been in a different life. She imagined Piper, Tegan and Felix here at the party as a family, with Alice and George still somehow in their lives. Happy together, celebrating each other, loving each other, no one having to lose out. She imagined herself sipping champagne with Piper, affectionately sharing stories about Tegan, stroking Felix's soft, downy head tenderly, both of them loving their girl. An affectionate auntie, distant but not forgotten. Just one big family.

Knowing this was never going to happen, Alice pushed away this fanciful dream, then saw Becka and Charlie, and waved. Becka grinned, pulling away from a conversation with a young woman Alice hadn't met before, holding the hand of a blonde little girl, who looked about five years old. Alice's heart ached briefly for Tegan, as she realised the child must be Parker and Phoenix's sister, Bonnie. Biting down on any feelings of jealousy or sadness for herself and George, Alice thought resolutely that it was so lovely that she and her parents were here.

Becka, collecting two glasses of pink champagne from a tray on the table, was heading towards Alice now. She looked beautiful in a lilac summer dress, her hair freshly dyed blue, falling in curls over her shoulders, tattoos on show.

'Boys, here's Auntie Alice!' she cried before pulling her friend into a tight hug. Parker and Phoenix, dressed adorably in matching shorts, shirts and braces, ran over and immediately demanded to be lifted up. And the two women, laughing, put down their champagne before they'd even taken a sip to do so. Alice squeezed Parker tightly and placed a kiss on his soft, blond head, loving the sweet cuddles he and his brother gave so freely now the attachments to their mums were firmly established.

Alice recalled Becka's concerned words on the phone the week before. 'Are you sure you want to come? Of course, we'd completely understand if you felt you couldn't. Do what's right for you, Alice. The last thing we want is to make things harder for you. We love you and George, you know?'

But there was no question of not going. Despite everything, Alice had looked forward to this party for weeks, desperate to see her friends and their children. That morning as she got ready, Alice could hear George, shoes and coat on, shouting up the stairs.

'Come on, love, we'll be late!'

Alice looked at her reflection a few moments longer in the dressing room mirror before applying one last coat of lipstick and glancing down at the text she'd just received.

Last week, it had been exactly a year since they'd returned from matching panel, excited that Tegan would come to live with them, and now, it was as though they'd come full circle. The sunshine yellow bedroom, so excitedly prepared for Tegan, now a dressing room filled with Alice's new clothes and neatly organised shoes.

She thought of the way the little girl had shyly said, 'Thank you, Alice. I've learned a lot from you and George, and I love all my new toys,' squeezing Alice in a brief, tight hug, before she had left to get in Peggy's car, walking out of Alice and George's home for the last time, leaving Alice both in awe and sadness at the maturity she'd seen in such a young girl.

And despite everything that had happened, and despite knowing that the best outcome had been found for Tegan, accepting that she was no longer a mother had been hard for Alice. Passing the closed door of the bedroom every day, knowing what had once lain behind it, was heart-breaking, so, repurposing the space into a sumptuous dressing room, repainted and new, was Alice's way of moving on.

Looking into the gilt-edged mirror, she realised she was a different woman than she had been a year before. Stronger in some ways, more vulnerable in others. If only she knew then what she knew now, thought Alice. It was the year my heart broke in two and was remade, never to be the same again.

Reading the text from Peggy, she smiled sadly:

'Hi Alice, hope you and George are well. Just to let you know Tegan is doing fine. Ups and downs as to be expected but doing well, all things considered. Sami's been to speak to her and talked to her about Piper, told her about the baby. Tegan is so excited. Wasn't sure how she'd react but seems happy to have a new brother. Tegan is seeing Piper and Felix next week for first time. Fingers crossed it goes well! Love to you both, Peggy.'

Alice closed the text, got up, and left the room, closing the door firmly behind her. Tegan was doing well. That text was a gift, a way of connecting to her almost-daughter, and Alice cherished every communication she received about her. After all this time, that was everything she could hope for. The child was happy and reunited with her family.

And now it was time for Alice to do the same. Running down the stairs, she pulled on her shoes, ready to leave for the party, picking up gifts as they left the house.

This party represented a huge milestone in the lives of the couples. The celebration of finally, legally, becoming families. Parker and Phoenix's adoption order had been granted promptly by the courts due to the sad death of Keira just a few months before. She had no family to claim the boys, and the courts were quickly convinced that Becka and Charlie were the best parents for them.

Adrian and Michael had a slightly longer, more worrying wait when Joey's birth father had turned up at court at the last minute to contest, but in the absence of any evidence to show his life had changed, the judge had finally ruled in the men's favour just a couple of months later.

So now Parker, Phoenix and Joey were legally part of their new families and it was time to celebrate the end of the adopters' journey to approval and the beginning of the rest of their lives with their children. Calling the three couples together on this beautiful summer's day, Adrian took Michael's hand and lifted his son onto his hip, tears evident in his eyes as the others raised their glasses.

'I just wanted to say such a big thank you to you all!' he said. Then, looking at Alice and George, he carried on, 'I know this year has been such a huge one for all of us, but Michael and I just wanted to say that we couldn't have done this without your support. We're a family now, and us, well, we're friends forever, aren't we?'

'I'll drink to that!' said Charlie, as Michael popped the cork on a fresh bottle of champagne, the friends were cheering and hugging, with their boys – Parker, Phoenix and Joey – squeezed between them.

'Hear, hear!' said Becka.

Alice looked at all of her friends and their gorgeous children, children she loved and would spoil as her own. Holding George's hand, she gave thanks for their love and the friends they had around them, their wonderful chosen family. Alice didn't know what was in store for her and George, but she did know they'd already faced their greatest fears, and whatever came next couldn't phase her. For now, all the love she had would go to George, her friends, their beautiful children, and the excitable new puppy she and George had introduced cautiously to their older dog, Mitch, the week before.

And, she thought, she has a secret.

Something she was keeping close to her heart, just for a while, wanting to wait until they got home before disclosing it to George. But for now, it was just hers, and she guarded it like the most precious gift. Her new role. Appointed earlier that afternoon when Becka took her by the hand, pulling her into the kitchen, away from the crowd.

Holding both of Alice's hands, Becka's words rushed out.

'We're having a naming ceremony for the boys, you know, now the adoption order is finalised. Now they're ours! And, well, it would be a huge honour for us if you and George would agree to be "guide-parents" for the boys? Charlie and I really want you in their lives, and they love you two so much. Please say yes!'

Alice didn't need to say anything, just nodded as tears filled her eyes and she squeezed her friend tight. She couldn't think of anything more special to come into her life, just as she needed it, and it filled her up with gratitude for her friend who seemed to know exactly how to help.

Pushing away tears before they threatened to spill over, she grinned widely at Becka. 'I think it's time for cake!' she said as they re-joined the party.

It was at that moment that Alice knew, surrounded by her friends and all of this love, that they'd be okay. Alice and George. Husband and wife, dog parents, friends and guideparents to two beautiful boys.

And stepping out into the sunshine, she looked over at her husband and smiled. Her heart may still be aching, but somehow, she knew that there in the cracks, it was beginning to also fill up with something new. A kind of tentative hope for the rich and beautiful future she and George would make for themselves. A different future than the one they'd imagined, but one that could be special all the same.

Alice's blog

NOW

By the time you read this, I will no longer be a mummy. The most difficult of decisions has brought my journey to parenthood to a close. It's taken me three long days to write this and longer to be able to post it. I hope you will read and understand just how hard it has all been.

In the beginning, there was the becoming. You were there with me, holding my hand along each step of the way. My cheerleaders, how I needed you to hold me up. Much like giving birth, our fertility journey was exhausting and painful. It tested us in every way possible. Physically and emotionally, we were drained. But, unlike those who experience childbirth, we came to the end of our road with nothing to hold. No tiny baby to make our family complete, to make all the pain finally worth it.

Adoption grew in our hearts like the light of hope at the end of a long, dark tunnel. We learned, we hoped, we prayed, and we shared our experiences with those going through a similar journey to us. We found a new community, and our journey of 'becoming' continued. We were becoming parents, still. My husband and I continued to hope against the odds that parenthood would find us in whatever way it could.

They told us about a beautiful girl who needed a home, and we opened our hearts to her. We so desperately wanted to be the parents she needed us to be and for her to be the child to complete our family.

The training took us through so much of what we would face, but it didn't prepare us for what was about to happen. It never braced us thoroughly enough for a child who was fiercely loyal to her birth family, who didn't want, or think she needed, a new family. A child who could never see us as Mummy and Daddy, no matter how hard we tried.

This child already had a mummy she loved very much. A mummy who was still very much alive and wanted above all else to be a parent to her own little girl.

There are so many heart-breaking reasons behind why a parent may not be able to care for their child or keep them safe. Finances, domestic violence, homelessness, lack of education, lack of support, and a history of childhood abuse are just some of them. For so many reasons, adoption is a beautiful, wonderful, life-changing gift for many children and families.

But, not being able to care for your child doesn't mean you no longer love them. Or they, you. And you should always have a chance to prove that you are strong. Drag yourself out of the circumstances that held you down and kept you from your child. Prove, despite everything that's gone before, that you can love and care for that child after all. Surely you should have a chance to do so!

We tried to love a child who wasn't ours, a child old enough to remember to whom she belonged. We tried to replace someone who was, to her, irreplaceable. They took away her mummy and told her she had to love a new mummy now, but she couldn't do it. And neither could I.

To force this child to accept me as her mummy, when she knew the one she wanted was still out there, would have sentenced us both to a lifetime of irresolvable difficulties. It would be like trying, every day, to push a square peg into a round hole and always wondering why it never fits.

And so, in the end, there was the unbecoming.

To 'unbecome' a mother to a living child is the most heart-breaking job in the world. The irony of this impossibly hard journey is that being a good parent, and making a decision that was in the child's best interests, means that I have ended up no longer being a parent at all.

Losing a child to miscarriage or to adoption breakdown might look different, but they're not. Not really. All of a sudden, the child is gone, and you're left wondering what went wrong. How could this happen? All the dreams for a future with that child leave with them, and you're left with an empty room and a broken heart.

They're gone, they're not coming back, and no one wants to talk about it. The loss of a child, a potential child, either through birth or adoption, is a pain and suffering like no other. And the spiralling feelings of grief, self-doubt, and failure are all-consuming.

I have experienced the feeling of having a foetus unable to thrive inside my body and a child who failed to thrive in my home, despite having created what I thought were the perfect conditions for them both. And this realisation that it wasn't enough, in either case, was an empty, cold kind of grief.

Three years after miscarrying twins, my husband and I sat and waited while the social workers arrived to move the girl who would have been our daughter to a new placement. We stared into an empty bedroom where she should have been, wondering where things had gone wrong.

Yes, I 'gave back' my child. And it was the most painful, selfless decision I've ever had to make in my life. But despite the pain, I know, without doubt or regret, that it was the only decision I could have made. I gave my daughter back to be with her mother because fighting to keep them apart was doing nothing but causing us all unbearable pain.

After all of the sadness I went through to become a mother, I finally succeeded. Then I gave my daughter back, and as I write this, the best of friends do what I would previously have believed to be the unthinkable – they quietly pack away her tiny clothes in the bedroom I painted just for her.

My friends have loved me throughout it all, holding me up with their unconditional friendship and support, without ever once questioning my decisions, and for that, I am enormously grateful.

I can make hard decisions, but I can't pack up her things. I have to say goodbye to her in my own way.

I will remember her giggle and cheeky smile. And I hope her mother gets to see them again. I know she'll keep them close to her heart, just like I will.

I unbecame a mother, and I will never be one again.

This is my story.

Acknowledgements

Writing this book has been a labour of love, and I couldn't have done it without the incredible support of my family and friends. I am always reluctant to write lists of thanks or gratitude for fear of inadvertently missing anyone out, but this is a non-exclusive list of thanks to all those who have supported me in bringing this book to life. My thanks go to everyone who has read it or encouraged me along the way!

Particular thanks go to:

The #ukadoptioncommunity and the #bookstagram community on Instagram who have continually and generously offered their wisdom, advice, empathy and understanding through some of the most challenging times as well as the joyous ones. I am endlessly thankful to you all for your community and support as my wife and I have built our family through adoption, and during the writing of this book.

David and Saskia and all of the team at New Generation Publishing for bringing my book idea to life and for the fantastic editing/proof-reading/critique services that helped to improve the final product!

Those who kindly read and provided me with so much support in the early drafts in particular Suzy Stanton (author of *The Adopter's Guide to Adoption*) and Rosemary Lucas (author of *The Family Fairies*).

To everyone who reads this book, thank you. I set out to write a book that I would have wanted to read, and I hope I have achieved that, and that in this book, all adopters, prospective adopters and those who have experienced the heart-breaking choices involved in adoption disruption find something that they can relate to and something that resonates with their journey. And for prospective adopters, I hope you find it inspiring and encouraging and all of my best wishes to you on your journey to building your family through adoption.

And finally, my wife and our children for just being them. For going out on long walks and bike rides on weekend mornings so that I could write and edit (and tear my hair out at times!), for bringing me cups of coffee and snacks, for providing the best tight hugs and being the best little family I could have ever hoped for.

All my love to you x

Printed in Great Britain
by Amazon